5/2018

WITHDRAWN

PRAISE FOR
THE TOYOTA ENGAGEMENT EQUATION

"In The Toyota Engagement Equation, *Tracey and Ernie Richardson achieve the remarkable feat of describing from their first days at Toyota the systematic Lean education they received—and they do so in a way that allows readers to grow alongside them. This is the education, particularly the* Lean thinking *behind Lean methods, that you need whether you are a team leader or a CEO, a director of continuous improvement, or a Lean coach. As I read chapter after chapter, I keep thinking that this is the education I wish I had received 30 years ago. I would have made (and written down) many fewer mistakes. You will too."*

—**JAMES P. WOMACK,** coauthor of *The Machine That Changed the World* and *Lean Thinking*, and founder of the Lean Enterprise Institute

"A brilliant and insightful firsthand account capturing how Toyota builds unique strengths through developing capabilities and growing leaders."

—**DANIEL T. JONES,** coauthor of *The Machine That Changed the World, Lean Thinking,* and *Lean Strategy*

"This terrific book from Toyota veterans Tracey and Ernie Richardson delivers the secret ingredient in Toyota's magic potion for enduring success: developing and nurturing people, carefully and patiently, to improve the business by creating a culture of problem-solvers, and achieving superior performance. They capture their lifelong learning experience in a simple but subtle formula that will change how you think about Lean and unlock the infinite potential of your people's talent and passion for continuous improvement."

—**MICHAEL BALLÉ,** coauthor of the Shingo Prize winning *The Gold Mine* trilogy and cofounder of Institut Lean France

"Tracey and Ernie continue Mr. Cho's vision to share wisdom with the next generation. Filled with knowledge gained from failures and successes inside Toyota and beyond. . . . illustrating their leadership in coaching and developing others striving to implement a Lean culture."

—**CHERYL JONES,** former Vice President of
Toyota Motor Engineering and Manufacturing,
North America, and founder of F1Help

"Tracey and Ernie have captured the most critical parts of what we learned at Toyota as well as the learning process. Equally important, they've shared their personal journeys in vivid detail, revealing how it was such a meaningful experience. I predict this book will become an invaluable resource for leaders and companies in their Lean and continuous improvement efforts."

—**DAVID VERBLE,** former North American Toyota
Manager, partner at Lean Transformations Group, and
coauthor of *Mapping to See* and *Perfecting Patient Journeys*

"Rarely do we get an in-depth view of how excellence is actually born. In this powerful book, Tracey and Ernie have captured the je ne sais quoi of how Toyota develops its people and manages its business in a literal page turner. You'll never view learning, leading, and achieving the same way again. Even better—this isn't merely a book for thinkers. This is a book for people who want to do and do well."

—**KAREN MARTIN,** author of *The Outstanding
Organization* and *Clarity First*

"This is undoubtedly the best book about Lean management that I've ever read. The experiences and situations that Ernie and Tracey share are key to understanding what's behind the Toyota DNA equation. This masterpiece allows readers to become immersed within the walls of Toyota, putting them in the shoes of Toyota's members and leaders."

—**JONATHAN ESCOBAR MARIN,** Director, Global Head
of Lean Management at HARTMANN GROUP, Partner at
HPO Global Alliance, and Cofounder and CEO at Inn-Be

THE TOYOTA ENGAGEMENT *EQUATION*

HOW TO UNDERSTAND AND IMPLEMENT CONTINUOUS IMPROVEMENT THINKING IN ANY ORGANIZATION

TRACEY RICHARDSON

ERNIE RICHARDSON

New York Chicago San Francisco Athens London Madrid
Mexico City Milan New Delhi Singapore Sydney Toronto

1 2 3 4 5 6 7 8 9   LCR   22 21 20 19 18 17

ISBN   978-1-259-83742-5
MHID   1-259-83742-4

e-ISBN   978-1-259-83743-2
e-MHID   1-259-83743-2

This publication is designed to provide accurate and authoritative information in regard to the subject matter covered. It is sold with the understanding that neither the author nor the publisher is engaged in rendering legal, accounting, securities trading, or other professional services. If legal advice or other expert assistance is required, the services of a competent professional person should be sought.
   —*From a Declaration of Principles Jointly Adopted by a Committee of the American Bar Association and a Committee of Publishers and Associations*

McGraw-Hill Education books are available at special quantity discounts to use as premiums and sales promotions or for use in corporate training programs. To contact a representative, please e-mail us at bulksales@mheducation.com.

To all the thinkers, learners, and influencers out there we have worked with over the years, thank you for evolving us to be the coaches we are today and will be tomorrow as we continue to learn and grow on our journey together!

~~ Go Thinking ~~

Contents

■ ■ ■

PART 3
Everybody Everyday Engaged

Foreword

■ ■ ■

My personal journey with Toyota's unique approach to management began in 1987 when I signed on as the 292nd hire at Toyota Motor Manufacturing of Kentucky (TMMK), the company's first wholly owned North American operation.

The Georgetown facility was still under construction and more than a year away from producing cars, so my earliest lessons came through participation in a thorough preparation process working at Toyota.

Building a manufacturing base in North America was a big leap for Toyota, and its leaders were determined to get it right. Consequently, they put their best people behind the project—individuals who continued to advance up through the ranks after they returned to Japan. This talented group was like a handpicked all-star team sent on a big mission, and they spent nearly a year preparing for the plant launch before they left Japan.

Prior to joining Toyota, I had been in quality management for 10 years and had risen to the role of division quality manager of an automotive supplier for three plants in North America. When I was offered the job at Toyota, my Toyota superiors had different ideas—they wanted me to walk back to the specialist (engineering) position so I could really learn the business from the basement floor all the way up through the organization. Taking two steps back like this seemed like a hard pill to swallow back in those young days in my career, but it was the best decision I ever made.

There was good reason for Toyota's approach. As I soon discovered, we were expected to spend a significant portion of our time developing people, so it was critical for us to have a deep understanding of the work we would be asking our people to do. Toyota's hiring strategy assured that there was a good mix of individuals with and without manufacturing experience. However, all members followed a common development path based on the principles and values that comprise Toyota's unique way of doing business.

We spent long days with our Japanese leaders in an atmosphere of discovery and experimentation, and many of the methods that we would use were under construction just like the factory. Training materials and textbooks were typically typed or handwritten, and provided only a basic overview—the real learning took place when our trainers walked us through the concepts on the actual production floor.

Concepts and methods, however, were only part of the story—there was also enormous emphasis on making sure that we fully appreciated the cultural foundation that was essential to the methods we were learning. This continued throughout my career at Toyota and often involved trips to Japan to see these concepts in action. The Toyota expression for such visits is "going to *gemba*," that is, going to the source to understand the facts through your own eyes. Many times we had to acquire an understanding of the concepts and then adapt them to work successfully in North America.

Toyota's culture has many elements, and these had a long history even then. For example, Toyota faced a financial crisis in 1949 resulting in severe restrictions on its ability to borrow money. Toyota's leaders concluded that the only path to growth was through their people. Consequently, they doubled down on the basics of respecting their team members and ensuring that the company, through its long-term success, would be able to provide sustainable employment. This led to a series of best practices, later known as the Toyota Production System, for assuring quality while minimizing waste in a Lean environment. The Toyota Way was then developed to ensure that every employee understood Toyota's unique way of doing business.

With that came the firm conviction that the company could never let its guard down. When things are going well in most companies, management and its employees will say, "Okay, we're making all kinds of money. We can relax." At Toyota, however, that's the point where people really hunker down and ask, "What can we do better in the future to improve quality, improve efficiency, or reduce costs?"

Embedding this thinking in the culture from day one was critical because the responsibility for solving problems and making improvements didn't just rest with process engineers or time study professionals. At Toyota, everybody must become a problem-solving expert at his or her level. Team members solve problems that are appropriate for team members to solve, team leaders solve team leader problems, and the pattern continues for supervisor problems, engineering problems, or senior manager problems. The result is a continuous chain of improvement activities that pervades the entire organization.

To maintain this, problems must be defined appropriately and simplified for all people to be able to solve them. For example, when accountants talk about cost per vehicle, they tend to refer to generalized cost categories such as consumables, raw materials, scrap, or energy. But it's very difficult for team members or team leaders on the floor to wrap their hands around that and support that improvement, and we want everyone to work on reducing costs.

The costs our team members can relate to are items like the gloves they use every day. If you are working on the interior of a vehicle, it's very important that you don't stain the surfaces with oily handprints or fingerprints, so gloves are necessary. Those gloves have a cost, and that cost is part of the cost of a vehicle.

The cost that the gloves add to each vehicle depends on how many vehicles we can build before we change our gloves. Let's say it's 100 vehicles. But if team members can find a way to increase that to 125 vehicles, maybe by not touching a dirty, oily part that goes into the suspension, or by separating the job where the interior people don't get their gloves dirty, they can extend the life of those gloves and reduce the cost. Maybe that's only 25 cents a car, but in an assembly plant where you may have 300 people working on the line building 200,000 cars per year, it adds up pretty quickly. This is just one simple example that illustrates how everyone in the organization can be involved.

In Toyota's culture, every employee is tuned into this kind of thinking, and understands how his or her role supports the entire organization, right up to the CEO. As leaders, it was our job to engage everybody in that way of thinking.

Respect for people was central to this, and that included an understanding that humans make mistakes. I learned about the significance of this early on when I made a poor judgment trying to understand a quality problem. This was understood to be part of the learning experience, and we were encouraged to take these opportunities to reflect on how to improve in the future. However, this time my reflection had to be reported to our president, Fujio Cho. I thought for sure that I was going to get terminated or at least reprimanded.

Based on the Toyota Way, I used Toyota's A3 format (which you'll learn all about in this book), which summarizes the problem-solving steps on a single 11 × 17 sheet of paper. I spent three days preparing my report, and when I arrived in Mr. Cho's office, my hands were wringing wet.

I sat in front of Mr. Cho and explained, "This is what happened, this is what I did, this is the gap, this is the problem I had, and this is what I plan to do next time." He listened patiently, and then folded the paper in half, sat back and folded his hands together, and said, "So what did you really learn from this event?"

And that was it. Clearly, I had learned quite a lot from the incident, but the respect that Mr. Cho showed me had a profound effect.

Years later, I was senior vice president, and we were in the start-up phase of the new plant in San Antonio, Texas. As the paint shop preparation was nearing completion, we were doing the initial fill of our paint system with chemicals and electro deposit (ED) paint in large metal tanks. We were just getting ready to run the process when I got a call on my radio, which was how we were communicating since the plant was under construction.

"Don, you have to visit this process," said the caller.

"What's going on?" I asked.

"You won't believe it when you see it," he said.

I came running to the process, and there were maybe 10 people circled around a team leader. I looked up in the air, and if you can imagine, it was like a bathtub, three stories tall, filled with green paint and overflowing at the top. It was dripping paint everywhere, all over the equipment.

As I approached the team leader, all the other employees took off, and this one team leader was left standing there. He had green paint all over his paint suit and hard hat.

Now, my first reaction was to think about the enormous costs and repercussions this was going to have. But then, all of a sudden, I had a flashback of my meeting with Mr. Cho years earlier.

So I walked up to the team leader and I said, "What happened?"

He said, "Well, I asked the paint supplier to support me in turning off the fill valve, but he forgot and went home."

I paused for a moment, and then I asked, "What did you learn today?"

He shared some of the lessons he had learned. For example, never transfer your job responsibilities to somebody else.

About a month later, I was out in the plant and I saw this team leader again. I asked him how his job was going, and he said everything was fine. I noticed that he was still wearing the hard hat with green paint all over it. I asked why.

"Because of the way you treated me," he said. "You respected me." Of course, he knew very well that in many organizations, that mistake would have cost him his job. At Toyota, I was able to say, "No, that's part of the development process." And when people asked who was responsible for the paint spill, I was able to say, "That's not what's really important—what matters is what we learned from the experience, and how we'll apply that to prevent similar incidents in the future."

Stories like this, which were common at TMMK, reveal a very different mindset from what most people are used to in their working environment. Every one of us, from the team member to senior management, was trained to think and act differently, and this pervaded all of our work.

Therefore, when describing Toyota's approach to people in other organizations, it's critical to get people at all levels to understand that culture is based on a common belief and common direction, and that it's up to management to totally engage the entire organization in a continuous improvement mindset with a clear focus on company objectives.

Tracey and Ernie Richardson, my former Toyota colleagues and fellow Kentuckians, are devoted teachers who understand this deeply. I had the opportunity to work with both of them, and they are great examples of people who embraced the Toyota development process and became experts in their respective areas. Today, they use their knowledge and wisdom to support other organizations in the areas of continuous improvement, leadership development, and the essence of problem solving at all levels of the organization.

Tracey and Ernie have developed a simple theme that any business can use to move forward on the path to improvement, and that theme forms the basis of this book. Through this lens and numerous accounts of their experiences at Toyota, they reveal the essence of the continuous improvement mindset that has been so essential to Toyota's success. Their approach is both highly practical and deeply personal. As you read the pages ahead, be prepared to be entertained, enlightened, and changed forever.

I would like to join Tracey and Ernie in thanking all of the trainers, coordinators, and managers at TMMK for their initiative in providing new manufacturing jobs, and for the priceless wisdom that they shared with us so generously. I would also like to commemorate Kieta Takenami, my former coordinator, who lost his life in a tragic airplane crash in Detroit. I was waiting at the airport to pick him up, but he never made it. Fortunately, his legacy, and that of Toyota's many wonderful teachers, lives on through the thousands of people who bring these unique principles and values to their daily work, their lives, and their communities.

DON JACKSON, Jackson Management Group, LLC
Past Senior Vice President, Toyota Motor Manufacturing, and
past President of Manufacturing, Volkswagen North America

Acknowledgments

■ ■ ■

This book is the result of many combined decades of living and breathing the Toyota Way of thinking. We both are thankful for all the priceless opportunities and experiences Toyota Motor Manufacturing provided us over the years.

I would like to start off with a heartfelt thank you to my husband Ernie for helping me see this dream through to its end form. I look forward to continuing our journey of leading and learning together, and sharing our wisdom with those we are blessed to work with.

Ernie and I want to share how grateful we are to have worked under the leadership of Mr. Fujio Cho when he was president at TMMK during the start-up phase. Thank you, Mr. Cho, for modeling Go to See, Ask Why, and Show Respect for People each day for us. Your thinking has been a guiding beacon for us all these years, and we continue to pass that shared wisdom to the next generation.

We were influenced by so many trainers, coordinators, executive coordinators, executives, and presidents during our time at TMMK that it's impossible to name them all. However, we'd like to give special thanks to Don Jackson, Pete Gritton, Russ Scaffede, Mike Hoseus, Dewey Crawford, and David Meier, who all provided input for this book. Thanks also to Noboru Hidaka, Shigeru Goda, Shoichi Ikoma, Shigeo Takahashi, Osamu Ito, Gary Convis, and Wil James for their leadership and the influence that they had on our thinking. We would like to also commemorate Nobukazu Fujii and Dave Downs, who were wonderful mentors and supporters.

I would like to thank Mike Hampton and Evelyn Mitchell White for their friendship and support when we were early hires in the Plastics department at TMMK. Ernie would like to thank his Powertrain colleagues Ken Anderson, Catesby Prewitt, and Tim Spencer for their support over the years.

A special thank you to Jacob Stoller for collaborating with us to gather and document our thoughts throughout the journey of writing this book, and to Jon Miller for helping us develop the vision that got this book off the ground.

We'd like to thank our editor, Donya Dickerson, editorial director at McGraw-Hill Education, for her enthusiasm and support, as well as Knox Huston, formerly with McGraw-Hill Education, who first read our proposal and gave us the opportunity to share our story all over the world.

We've had the opportunity to lead and learn with many wonderful people in our sessions and would like to give particular thanks to the following who provided input for this book: Peter Ward, Al Mason, Scott Powell, Brian Kettler, Kelly Moore, Frank Wagener, Vicente Ramirez, Deanna Hall, Alan Kandel, Paul Trahan, Bret Kindler, Tanya Doyle, and Fran Vescio.

A special thank you to John Shook, chairman and CEO of the Lean Enterprise Institute, for contributing your wisdom in the book, and for everything we've learned from you and your team at the Lean Enterprise Institute over the years.

I would like to recognize my mother and father for always seeing the potential in me. You set great examples over the years with your work ethic and long careers at the University of Kentucky and IBM. You both always gave 110 percent to help me become the person I am today. Special thanks also to my grandparents who always supported my vision and dreams, especially my late maternal grandfather, who worked 42 years at General Electric as a foreman. He read the early chapters I had put together back in 2007 and said, "This is really going to be special!" And finally, a very special thank you to my younger sister Ashley for always being there for me as a best friend and supporter in life.

Introduction

■ ■ ■

Our purpose for writing this book is to share what we learned as Toyota employees during a very special event in history—the start-up years of Toyota Motor Manufacturing of Kentucky (TMMK), Toyota's first wholly owned North American factory.

This was a watershed moment for Toyota—here the company was establishing a foothold in the world's largest and most competitive market. To ensure success, Toyota's leaders exceeded even their own high standards for developing people.

As many readers are aware, Toyota was also engaged in a joint venture with General Motors called New United Motor Manufacturing (NUMMI). In that initiative, Toyota brought its production methods to a troubled GM plant in Fremont, California, to help turn that operation around. Production in the restructured plant had begun a year before we rolled our first cars off the line in 1988, and the factory eventually became one of the most efficient GM plants in the United States.

TMMK was very different. Rather than working with an existing organization and infrastructure, Toyota set out to build and equip a factory, establish its own supply chain and sales networks, and most important, develop its own workforce. The objective wasn't just to make sure the new employees could build cars—we were also seen as the future leaders that the company would depend on to grow the North American organization. And as we were to learn later, our region, known as the Horse Capital of the World, was chosen in part for a workforce that had very few preconceived ideas about manufacturing. From that perspective, they couldn't have made a better choice!

The scope and quantity of training we received, therefore, far exceeded the normal boundaries of corporate training—our classroom hours were equivalent to a full-time university program, and the course content was extremely demanding.

But even more important, Toyota allocated phenomenal resources to the program. During the months leading to the start-up of production, the company brought hundreds of trainers over from Japan on rotating assignments, some of whom had learned in the presence of Taiichi Ohno and his colleagues. Our trainers were highly respected in Japan, and they had the time and the freedom to share their wisdom generously—often on a one-to-one basis.

What stood out in their approach is that they didn't just teach methods—they wanted to make sure that we understood the "why." Therefore, when we were working through a set of prescribed steps, they often would ask, "What were you thinking?" As we discovered over time, helping us understand the *thinking* behind the methods was the most important aspect of instilling the unique Toyota culture in a North American facility.

Our training, therefore, resembled what an apprentice receives when learning a trade from a master. The emphasis was on learning by doing and teaching by example. The "classroom" was usually the factory floor, and our textbooks, if they existed at all, were either typed or handwritten. Usually, we learned through the spoken word and visual demonstrations, sometimes with the help of a translator. And as you will see in the many stories in the book, our trainers preferred to teach by asking questions and challenging us to find our own answers even if they sensed we might initially get it wrong.

However, this wasn't just about them training us. Toyota's leaders were keen to learn about American culture, which they admired in many respects. And in fact, it turned out that many of the lessons our leaders learned in Kentucky influenced the practice of the Toyota Way back in Japan. And Fujio Cho, who headed TMMK in those early years, went on to serve as CEO of the Toyota Corporation from 1999 to 2005.

IT DIDN'T HAVE A NAME

As career employees of Toyota, we are often asked to reveal the "true meaning" of various words that have become part of the Lean vocabulary. The truth is, those particular words weren't used at Toyota. In fact, when we started in 1988, the term *Lean* had just been coined, and the Lean tools that are so familiar to us today were still being developed.

Therefore, when it came to describing our approach, we didn't call it anything. It was just understood that this was our J-O-B. It wasn't until Toyota documented the Toyota Way in 2001 that words, labels, and so forth surfaced—and surged. This was a necessary step for maintaining Toyota's values, principles, and methods in a growing global organization, but it's important to remember that labels have limitations, particularly when it comes to creating something as intimate as Toyota's work culture. The danger here is falling into the "tools only" approach that's all too common in organizations that seek to emulate Toyota.

From our viewpoint, we are not sure that any labels—and above all what newcomers derive from such labels—can ring true with what we learned through experience. That's a huge reason why calling this *anything* other than our J-O-B can have a hindering effect on a company trying to implement this thinking process. And it is an important reason why we wanted to share our experience in this book.

To convey the true spirit of Toyota's philosophies, we have made every effort to describe what it was like to learn these lessons through the voice of our Japanese trainers. It wasn't just what they said that mattered, it was how they said it and why. And although they were just learning English, the meaning behind their words was powerful and unforgettable. We still use some of their metaphors today.

We've also included comments and stories from some of our mentors, who worked with us in our early days, and remained friends after we had moved on to found our company, Teaching Lean Inc. Their insights, included in text boxes throughout the book, provide additional perspectives on a common experience that changed our lives. In a similar fashion, a number of our clients have provided comments on how they are applying the knowledge that we have been so privileged to pass on to them.

LEADING AND LEARNING

If you look at the Toyota Production System simplistically, it's about making problems and improvement opportunities visible to workers and management, and addressing them as close to the source as possible. Consequently, there was enormous transparency, and we were all taught the specific *thinking* for solving problems as they arose during our daily production.

In keeping with this philosophy, we soon discovered that we didn't have bosses in the traditional sense. Instead, Toyota used the servant leader approach in which leaders develop and support their people in a learning environment. We were accountable, therefore, to leaders who visited our *gemba* often, not to criticize or give orders, but to teach us. Although our leaders, all the way up to our president, Fujio Cho, made a point of studying a bit harder in order to remain one step ahead of us, they were not ashamed to admit that they didn't have all the answers, and sometimes we would be learning together. We were all like sponges back then, soaking in information from every facet of a rapidly evolving work environment.

A phrase often repeated at TMMK was "leading and learning." The idea was that people should always be learning and improving their thinking as they go, but at the same time developing others. This way of managing, along with a relative lack of a command and control hierarchy, will sound paradoxical to a student of traditional top-down management. If workers aren't told what to do, how can we ensure that they will put in their best efforts? And how can we ensure that they will work toward results that align with the company's goals?

The short answer is that in Toyota's workplace culture, employees not only manage themselves, but work in autonomous teams to help the company move forward toward its goals and toward the interests of the customer. Creating that culture is the primary focus of Toyota's philosophy and the precept behind the phrase "Toyota develops people who happen to build cars."

This culture has, in our view, two pillars—the *discipline* to follow a path of continuous problem solving and self-improvement, and *accountability* to work standards, fellow team members, company goals, and the customer experience. However, we didn't see these as two separate elements. Somehow they were both interwoven as a single entity that pervaded our daily work. For us, they represented the feeling of the Toyota culture that was atmospheric.

Therefore, we like to speak of discipline and accountability as one, and we have labeled the concept *DNA*, which is derived from "D 'n' A." In our years of training, DNA has been our brass ring. Every year, we try to get better at helping companies grasp and attain DNA, which in our view is the key to

Toyota's phenomenal achievements. And that is our goal with this book as well.

The leaders at TMMK brought this mindset to the workplace in two ways:

- They ensured that every worker learned and internalized both the skill set and the thinking for uncovering and addressing problems and improvement opportunities.
- They made sure every worker was engaged throughout the organization.

To reflect this, we organize our training programs around a simple learning equation, which is designed to help learners remember and internalize the essential elements that took us years of practice to assimilate.

$$GTS^6 + E^3 = DNA$$

GTS^6 represents six competencies required by every worker to identify and correct problems, and E^3, short for Everybody Everyday Engaged, represents the role of leaders in motivating and serving the workforce. The result is DNA. We will introduce the formula in detail in Part 2.

The formula should not lead one to believe that we are presenting instant answers. On the contrary, this book is about recapturing the *thinking* behind the tools that we feel often gets lost when people pursue a Lean agenda. That is why it has been so important for us to try to replicate the voices of our trainers, and to try to put you, the reader, in the same frame of mind we were in when we learned these lessons for the first time.

How to Use This Book

In our work as trainers and consultants, we find that our learners have a wide variety of needs. Some are discovering Toyota's methods for the first time. Others have mastered the Lean tools and want to better understand the culture behind them. In many cases, our participants are leaders who hope to recreate the *thinking* behind Toyota's methods in their organizations.

This book was written with all our learners in mind. We believe that the lessons from our trainers are timeless and universal. This is not a set of production tricks, nor is it a scheme for strategic management. It is a set of philosophies that apply at all levels of the organization, and at all stages of an organization's horizontal and vertical development. Even within an organization as large as Toyota, there is one Toyota Way.

Consequently, this is not a "Lean tool guide." Instead, it is a guide to the philosophies that override any tool-related considerations. Our trainers didn't talk about tools much, and we don't mention them very often in this book either.

We have organized the book into three parts. Part 1 tells, through our personal stories, how Toyota established its unique work culture in Georgetown, Kentucky. Part 2 describes the six problem-solving mindsets that make up the first half of the DNA equation. Part 3 describes the engagement practices that make up the second part of the DNA equation.

As we begin, we would ask you as reader to consider how these lessons apply to your work and your organization. Please read this book reflectively and with an open mind. Some of the ideas take some getting used to at first, and all require significant mental effort to master. Remember, this book is the result of the many years we spent at Toyota, and another eight years of reflection on how to pass this knowledge on.

With that in mind, let's get started!

Leading and Learning in Georgetown, Kentucky

"Before you say you can't do something, try it."
—SAKICHI TOYODA

1

The Phone Call

■ ■ ■

I n March of 1988, when I (Tracey) was 19, I received a phone call that forever changed my life. The caller was a human resources manager at Toyota's new Kentucky plant offering me a position as a production team member in the Plastics department. I wouldn't trade that call for anything in the world. This was not only a highly sought-after job, but the beginning of a journey of discovery that was to shape my entire career as a worker, learner, manager, and teacher of others.

My quest to join Toyota had begun nearly two years earlier when my father learned that the company was building a plant in nearby Georgetown and suggested that I apply there. Coming from a factory background, he understood what a rare opportunity this was, particularly given the economic challenges in our region. So I threw my name into the hat, not knowing what would become of it. As it turned out, it would be almost a year before I heard back from Toyota.

At the time, I had just graduated from high school, and I had decided, like some of my friends, to continue my studies at nearby Eastern Kentucky University (EKU) in the fall.

High school had been a mixed experience for me. I often describe myself as a hybrid between a kinesthetic learner and a visual learner, meaning I learn best through hands-on activity and visual information. Memorizing from books and lectures, on the other hand, didn't come naturally to me, so for courses that emphasized this kind of learning, I developed an adapting strategy where I'd find ways to learn the materials in my own kinesthetic/visual way. This got me through school with decent marks, but I never learned to study in the "classic" sense.

At EKU, I faced a very different learning environment. Most first-year courses were lecture-based, so without the traditional studying skills, I was at a considerable disadvantage. To compound this, professors weren't nearly as personal and accommodating as my high school teachers, and since I was living away from home for the first time, I no longer had the disciplined structure that my parents had provided. My first year at EKU, therefore, was a difficult one.

Then, as I was signing up for the fall semester of my second year, I got a phone call from a representative of the Toyota assessment process. The caller wanted to know if I was interested in taking the first level of testing in Lexington, which was the beginning of the screening process for potential new hires. I immediately said, "Yes I am. Tell me where I need to be and when, and I will be there with bells on!"

This was such an exciting moment for me that I wanted to scream out loud with joy and call as many people as I could think of to share the news. I was being offered a chance to compete for a highly coveted career opportunity, and it couldn't have come at a better time!

I was not, however, without concerns about giving up college. Part of me wanted to stay to prove that I really could succeed after a rough start. But I also believed that our paths are there to find, and Toyota seemed to be calling my name very loudly.

My parents, fortunately, were very supportive. College wasn't necessarily the only path for me, they pointed out, and would remain an option even if I did get hired by Toyota. Both had enjoyed successful careers without graduating from college: my father worked his entire career at IBM, and my mother rose to become director of student housing at the University of Kentucky. For them, the key to success had been a strong work ethic instilled in them by their parents, which emphasized discipline, determination, and gained experience. I feel blessed for the mentorship and support that they and my grandparents provided during those formative years.

I was reminded of our family work gene in 2001 when I read Kiichiro Toyoda's comment in *The Toyota Way* about his father, Toyota's founder Sakichi Toyoda: "My father was not educated. The only strength he had was to believe in one thing all the way."

I was extremely fortunate to find a company that truly valued the legacy that I had inherited from my family.

A NATURAL CHOICE

John Shook, Chairman and CEO, Lean Enterprise Institute

In the 1980s, Toyota was one of many Japanese manufacturers setting up shop in North America. Inside Japan, Toyota had a reputation for being somewhat slow and bureaucratic, and having a very strong culture. It was also known as the company from "there"—a remote farming region outside of Nagoya where people had a strong work ethic, but were considered unsophisticated compared to, say, workers in the fashionable Tokyo region where Nissan operated.

So Toyota was quite comfortable setting up in a rural area, and several remote sites were considered. Since Georgetown, Kentucky, was located right on the I-75 north-south auto supply chain corridor, it made perfect sense.

ROUND ONE

When I applied to Toyota, I had no experience with the hiring process of a large company, let alone one with the intensity Toyota had. So I was extremely nervous when I walked into the employment office in downtown Lexington for the first time, not sure what to expect, but also very eager to succeed so I could move on to the next round of testing.

After signing in, we were led into a back room where there were several setups for manual dexterity tests. For me, this was a good starting point. I had very good hand-eye coordination, which I had demonstrated as a player on school basketball teams through elementary, middle, and high school. I was also a proficient bowler—I had represented Kentucky in the national finals in 1984 and gone on that year to rank ninth in the United States. So I was eager to take on those physical tests, and as you can imagine, I had strong competitive instincts.

The dexterity tests centered around speed and quality. The first involved moving colored pegs on a peg board and flipping them over, and a number of other tests followed. All of them were timed, and although they were not overly difficult, I found that it required continual focus and concentration to maintain quality as my speed increased. As we progressed, the tasks began to feel natural to me, and by gauging my finish times, I figured I was in the top 10 percent of the group. "I could be successful at this company if given a chance to prove myself," I remember thinking at the time.

Next, we moved to a classroom-like situation for a "Situational Judgment Test or Inventory" (SJI). This was mostly multiple-choice and featured hypothetical questions such as the following:

- You are a team member online and you notice a defect on the car, and it wasn't a part you were responsible for. What would you do?

■ If you noticed a fellow team member working without gloves on their process, would you report them?

At the end of the session, the staff asked us to fill out an application for a team member position in production. We were told that we would be contacted if we qualified for the next round, which consisted of two 7-hour days of simulated work exercises in nearby Frankfort. I left there feeling pretty good about my chances, and I hoped I would hear back from them.

CONFRONTING A TOTALLY DIFFERENT WAY OF THINKING

Russ Scaffede, Former Vice President and General Manager, Powertrain, Toyota Motor Manufacturing Kentucky

If you worked for General Motors, you could take three-day tours of the NUMMI plant, which was the joint venture between GM and Toyota. We had internalized Toyota pretty well from a tool perspective, but when we saw NUMMI, we knew something was different. We couldn't put a finger on it, but it was totally different than what we had seen before.

MOVING CLOSER TO TOYOTA

Qualifying for the next round of tests was a major step up in a very competitive process. So those phone calls were highly coveted, and when I got the call inviting me to the next round, I was ecstatic.

As I was to learn later after I became a leader at Toyota, the company was looking for people who could handle the demanding task of production, but also thrive in an environment where you always have to be thinking and solving problems.

These additional qualities were especially critical because Toyota wasn't just looking for car builders—they needed people who could help them build the organization. As it turned out, I was employee number 1,428 (Ernie was 856) in an organization that now employs over 350,000 in North America.

DAY ONE

On the 30-mile drive to Frankfort, Kentucky, on the morning of the next round of tests, I was full of nervous anticipation. What would this round of tests be like? Would people be talking to me in Japanese? When I arrived at the sign-in area, I found that my fellow candidates were just as nervous and puzzled as I was.

Day one was about leadership, communications, and solving problems as part of a team. For the first exercise, I was put in a group of 12 people who all had various personality types, and I'm pretty sure this was intentional. The assessor gave us a list of 10 options typically found on vehicles, and our task was to rank them by priority.

The group dynamics were tricky here. The assessors, it appeared to me, were looking for leadership skills as well as our ability to deal with a person who may have favored the domineering trait, as well as one less talkative. I felt like I was trying to surface as one of the leaders, yet trying to be the one who was listening and giving input at the same time. I knew if I sat there and was too quiet, it may not have been in my best interest, so I forced the extrovert out and interjected as I felt necessary.

Some of the items were straightforward: it didn't take long to agree that headlamp washers were low priority. But when it came to a CD player (yes, this was the 1980s), we were getting into the gray area of personal preferences, so there was some disagreement.

I can remember being very uneasy during this activity, hoping things wouldn't get too out of control on the members' part, and that we all could work together as a team. A few people were very difficult to talk with and were determined to get their way. I have often wondered if those difficult people were planted there to "spice up" the conversation within each group. I guess we may never know.

I was sure, though, that "winning the discussion" was not the way to win a position at Toyota. Sensing this, I did my best to be neutral with a little aggressiveness toward accomplishing the task. I wanted to show I could work with others without being too judgmental, and also show my ability to be an influential part of the team.

CHOOSING THE RIGHT PEOPLE

Pete Gritton, Former Vice President of Human Resources, Toyota Engineering and Manufacturing, North America

When it came to hiring the right people, it was really all about the culture, although we weren't necessarily using that term at the time. We talked about what we needed from our people to be successful. They didn't necessarily have to have a high school diploma, but they needed basic reading, writing, and math skills, and they needed to be able to think logically and critically, and to come into our plant and think about how they do their work and how they could do it better.

The other big cornerstone was the ability to survive in a team environment where ideas are shared openly. It was about being open-minded, and being able to respectfully engage in constructive conversations about how to do things better. There were some subtle dynamics here. We didn't want the "I'm the big shot, and I'm going to take charge" kind of person, but we also didn't want the wallflower who just hangs back and lets others do the talking and engaging.

The second day of tests took place in a simulated production environment. Our first "product" was an assembly of plumbing pipes in a T-shaped format. There were several quality specifications that we had to meet before placing them in the finished product area. This was really my first experience with any production-oriented work.

We worked in 15-minute intervals with an assessor who observed our work as we built our pipes to the specifications. Our assessors tested us on speed and our ability to maintain consistent quality. It soon became clear, however, that they were looking for more than results—they also wanted to know *how* we achieved them. Did we follow a good process to get results consistently, or were we relying on luck?

Another twist was that the work environment was purposely set up with many inefficiencies. The assessors were looking for our ability to follow standardized work, but also solve problems that we were confronted with in the work environment. This was the beginning of my journey to see waste, or non-value added work, and my first glimpse at the foundations of the Toyota Production System.

After several hours of production, we took a break and then were given the opportunity to offer suggestions as to how we would make improvements to the work area. Being inexperienced, I was all over the map here—my ideas included parts layout redesign, tilting of the boxes for ergonomics, flow rack improvements, working with a radio on, and sequence of build to follow. I even suggested gloves since my fingers and hands were getting a little "worn"!

As it turned out, there were challenges ahead for my sore fingers. The next production sequence was even tougher, but I was determined and hung in there. Again, we were asked how we would improve the process. Looking back, I'm sure I missed lots of *kaizen* opportunities, but I had done well enough to make it to the next round.

THE INTERVIEW

Getting the call for the interview, which came in early 1988, was big news in itself—I couldn't decide which family member to call first! Many people at that time were very much hoping for a phone call like this, so I considered myself very blessed for being selected over thousands of applicants.

This was my first visit to the Toyota plant itself. It was one of those unforgettable moments, walking into the beautiful main lobby, realizing at the same time how important this could be for me. I was asked by the receptionist to take a seat and wait until my name was called. Rather than sit and worry, I had a good look at the scaled model of the Toyota campus that was on display in a glass case.

However, by the time my name was called, I had started to sweat and my butterflies were flying full force. I was instructed to go down a hallway and enter the last room on the right. As I walked in, I saw two gentlemen dressed in Toyota uniforms with many papers in front of them. They introduced themselves to me, and we sat down to begin the interview.

The first interviewer was David Meier, who was a production group leader in the Plastics department at the time. David is now a close friend and colleague in the Lean consulting world, and coauthor of *Toyota Talent* and the *Toyota Way Fieldbook*. My second interviewer was one of the very first TMMK human resources managers, Dewey Crawford.

David and Dewey were very nice and put me at ease in the interview, allowing me to think carefully about all the questions they were asking. Some were situational questions about production scenarios and problems. What had I learned from previous experience, they wanted to know, that I could apply to make work easier? In a very supportive way, they were probing any experience I might have had with problem solving.

They then asked me to recall a situation where I had created an improvement at work. The example that stood out in my mind came from my job experience at a local Wendy's fast-food restaurant, where I had worked during my high school years to help with gas money and such. My shifts were mostly at night and on the weekends, and the drive-through became my specialty because I had a knack for getting people through quickly.

David asked me to explain how I was able to do that, and my answer to him, as he told me years later, proved to be a determining moment in my interview. I explained that I had devised a little system where I would look at the order on the screen the moment it showed up, and calculate the customers' change in the drive-through lane before they came to the window. 80 percent of the people pay in round dollar amounts, so if they had a ticket for $5.52, I would have the 48 cents change ready in my hand, so all I had to do was deal with the paper bills.

This proved to save a lot of time and was a practice that I taught others. I don't think I invented the idea by any means—I see it a lot today as I visit drive-through windows—but this did come out of my own initiative to make things easier, and that's what impressed David. As the Japanese always told us, it's the small *kaizen* ideas, and seconds saved, that make a big difference. And as we will see in Part 2, Toyota's success was won one second at a time.

I left the interview feeling very good about my prospects, even though there were a few things I wished I'd said. I'd done my best, and now the only thing I could do was wait for the call.

BUILDING SUCCESSFUL TEAMS AT TMMK

**David Meier, former Group Leader,
Toyota Motor Manufacturing Kentucky**

When TMMK started hiring, we had just come out of a recession, so there weren't a lot of jobs available locally. Japan was also seen to be way ahead of the U.S. in manufacturing, and everybody wanted to work there, so there were about 100,000 applications for 2,000 positions.

I was hired as a group leader on June 22, 1987, but there were six months of learning and planning before I began hiring my team members. So by the time I interviewed Tracey for a team member position in Instrument Panels, I had a pretty good idea of what kind of people I needed to be successful, even though we didn't know what daily life was going to be like once we started production.

95 percent of the people we interviewed had no manufacturing experience, including Tracey—we were getting bank tellers, dental assistants, PhDs, all kinds of people. I'd spent a month working the processes at Toyota in Japan as part of my training, so I knew how hard the work was. So my greatest concern was, is this person going to walk out because it's too hard, too hot, or too dirty? I also knew that motivation and aptitude for problem solving would be essential skills.

The initial screening was handled by the State of Kentucky Employment Office, so we didn't get involved until later on, and we only saw people who had made it through a long battery of tests and had really high test scores.

Nevertheless, we were working through a huge stack of files from HR, and I was doing literally hundreds of interviews. We had a scoring process to ensure fairness, and there was usually an HR person present to help with that. I was interviewing primarily for my Instrument Panels group, but if I saw skills that fit better into another group, I'd usually recommend the candidate to another group leader.

Tracey did very well, and a couple of things stood out. One came when we asked her to recall a time when she had recognized a situation at work and come up with an idea to improve it. To answer, she talked about how, working at the drive-through, she had noticed that when a person's bill was, say, $8.20, she would figure they were going pay with a $10 bill. So she'd have the change ready by the time they got to the window.

I thought that was pretty clever—this was an idea that I might not have come up with myself. I was also impressed by the fact that she really appreciated the importance of problem awareness and problem solving, and how that would boost the performance of the company. This is a big part of Toyota, and Tracey really stood out.

Another was her success in competitive bowling. I was a pretty decent bowler as a kid, but nothing like Tracey, who was ranked nationally. I know what kind of discipline that would have taken, so all in all, I could really see Tracey fitting in. And when Tracey got promoted to team leader, and then group leader, my judgment about her proved to be correct.

IN HINDSIGHT—WHAT THEY WERE LOOKING FOR

One of the perks of getting hired and eventually becoming a leader was finding out what all those assessors and interviewers were looking for. For example, I learned later from one of our assessors, Gene Childress, that the same competencies were tested multiple times so that no single test would determine the final evaluation. This allowed for the fact that different people might display those competencies in different ways.

Furthermore, our results were being evaluated within the context of the position that we were applying for. So this wasn't just "canned" institutional testing.

Gene also told me that Toyota didn't really know what to expect from the workforce but wanted to be sure that we demonstrated all of the competencies needed to be a contributing team member. When you consider that uncertainty, and the fact that we were the early hires who would shape the organization, you can see why Toyota went through such a long and thorough process. And given how successful the plant was, it's amazing how effective the process was.

Although Toyota listed them slightly differently, I use the following competency categories to summarize the skills that Toyota was assessing us for. These are also, by the way, competencies I recommend you look for if you want to develop a more robust hiring process.

- **Listening skills.** This one is *deceptively simple*. How effective are we at really listening, and how do we know this? Our first instinct is to share our opinion before someone is finished, or to come up with a rebuttal in our minds before someone is even finished talking. During the exercises, our assessors were watching carefully for the folks who were truly able to listen and absorb new information.
- **Problem-solving skills.** Problem solving is important in any organization, but Toyota looks for this ability in each and every worker. Having an army of problem solvers, as we will see later, was the reason we won the J.D. Power Gold Plant Quality Award after only a few years of operation. Our assessors sought out this competency through frequent questions about how we would improve the work, the layout, or the work area. Could we see abnormalities and come up with our own ideas to make things better?

■ **Teamwork.** The ability to work with others is often downplayed as a given, but it is deeply rooted in the Toyota Way, where every employee is an essential part of the team. In the team exercises, our assessors paid careful attention to our responses to ideas offered by others, and our general attitude and demeanor throughout the exercise. Could we work effectively with people who had different personalities?

■ **Initiative.** Definitions of initiative vary pretty widely. In our assessments, Toyota was looking for people who would go above and beyond in terms of *creating ideas* for improvement. It wasn't about staying late or working up a sweat—this was about finding ways to work smarter and understanding the essential nature of value-added work. Would we, they wanted to know, be self-motivated to think, learn, and improve our own work processes?

■ **Leadership.** The expectation was that leaders would be promoted from within, so our assessors were looking for our potential as "homegrown" leaders. All of the above competencies, of course, were essential. In addition, our assessors wanted to know if we could help others develop these competencies. Did we respect others and have faith in their ability to improve? Could we see facts and not make assumptions about people? Could we handle difficult situations? Could we "walk the talk" and be suitable role models for others? These were questions that our assessors were constantly asking themselves.

The bottom line, I think, is that we'll never be experts at everything, so we all have to be willing and able to learn constantly. I like to think of myself as a sponge. When we become leaders, we should look for this same quality in our team members and new hires. As a trainer today, this is never far from my thoughts.

2

Early Days at Toyota

■ ■ ■

My first day at work at Toyota was August 1, 1988. I still remember it as if it were yesterday, and I often share my recollections of those memorable first moments when people in our sessions ask, "What was it like?"

In the weeks leading up to that day, I had occasionally seen people in the Lexington area wearing red "Team Toyota" T-shirts. I loved the idea that they were identified as "team" members and wondered if I too would be given one of those coveted T-shirts on day one.

It turned out that I was, and I wore it with pride. Toyota made us feel very special on that first day, and that feeling has never gone away for Ernie or me. This was our introduction to a great company that has a truly phenomenal way of working with people, and was to influence our lives so profoundly.

After signing in, I, along with 75 other new hires, entered a large room called Multi-Purpose A. This was the same room where, many years later, I would spend many hours sharing knowledge with others as a trainer/contractor for TMMK, and would frequently reflect back on the beginnings of my Toyota journey.

We began with routine matters such as benefits and other HR-related items, and there was a lot of paperwork. What caught my attention was the hours: my shift was from 6:30 a.m. to 3:15 p.m. As one used to the college life of afternoon classes and sleeping in, I remember doing the math and thinking, "Wow, I'll have to get up at 4:30 a.m. to get to work on time—this is going to be a culture shift in more ways than one."

But I felt there was so much opportunity for growth and advancements here that I resolved right then and there to take responsibility for changing my habits—basically as a 19-year-old growing up really fast.

Our journey really started on the second day, when we began a two-week process that Toyota called Assimilation. Most of this took place in a classroom. Of course, they covered the basics—benefits, rules around excused absences, parking regulations, plant layout, organizational structure, etc.

However, the training went far beyond this and included fundamentals of the Toyota Production System, the company's values, safety and environmental expectations, *andons* (explained later in this chapter), on-the-job development, and a variety of subject matter that was essential to becoming a successful team member in production. I can remember being very attentive in class because I wanted to make a good impression on my team when I got to go to my group on the production floor.

We also learned about the structure of the organization, and just how important development of people was. Each team leader had an average of only five team members he or she was responsible for, and this ratio held true through each level of the organization, giving leaders sufficient time to develop and train their people.

During those two weeks we were also taken to the production floor to see various processes in Assembly as well as other production departments. The operation was much smaller than it is today, but even then it made quite an impression on me.

When I was first taken to the area in Plastics where I would be working, I remember walking along the way through Assembly and Body Weld as construction was still underway, and looking up into the rafters and seeing those cars hanging down, with workers underneath them practicing their standardized work. My immediate reaction was "Oh wow, will I be able to do that and meet all the expectations?" The complexity of building a car and following such rigid standardized work seemed overwhelming, and my wide-eyed gaze must have spoken volumes. These days, I enjoy hearing from folks that shared that same amazed look when visiting the plant on public tram tours.

My first real day of work with my group began when my group leader, David Meier, picked me up and took me to lunch at the cafeteria near the Plastics department. (As you will remember, David had been one of my interviewers months before.) After lunch, David took me to meet my group, who were preparing at the time for our role in building trial instrument panel parts leading up to live production.

When I arrived at my new home in the plant with David, the group had made a big sign welcoming me as the newest member of the IP (Instrument Panel) Trim team. I was thrilled by the thought that I would soon be making, inspecting, and repairing that part of the vehicle.

After the warm welcome and introductions, I felt like I had joined a family. Everyone was so nice and team oriented, and wanted to make sure I knew all about the area. It was also clear that they were as ecstatic as I was about having been hand selected to build our Kentucky Camrys.

MY LEARNING JOURNEY
GOES INTO HIGH GEAR

As I mentioned earlier, TMMK was at a start-up stage when I signed on as a team member. We were all on a steep learning curve, and as the first day of producing cars that people were actually going to buy grew nearer, we were anxious about making sure we got everything right, and at the same time, excited about the events we were about to be a part of.

I didn't realize this at the time, but what I learned in those early months was pivotal to my success. It was here that I had my first in-depth learnings about standardized work, visualization, visual controls, problem solving, *kanban*, and TPS, to name a few.

Initially, much of this was handling physical production tasks in a standardized way, and some of it was very specific. I remember that there was a defined process for removing the excess foam from a right-hand steering column pad. We took pride in how we conducted these tasks, and it gave us a feeling of ownership of our jobs. Soon, we would be learning multiple jobs, and once the production levels warranted it, we would be rotating jobs to adjust for varying circumstances.

To make sure we covered all the necessary ground in our learning journeys, we used multifunctional worker charts similar to the one displayed in Figure 2.1.

My most profound learning of that time came from my first TMMK trainer, Mr. Shigeo Takahashi. Takahashi-san had come from Japan to train us, and he had very deep knowledge of the finer points of the Toyota Production System and standard work setups in Plastics. But more important, Takahashi-san had a deep understanding of the more granular aspects of values, teamwork, and reflection. This was personal development in a real sense of the word.

In general, the Japanese trainers from Toyota were very disciplined, with a strong sense of pride and ownership in what they did. Their way of working with us reflected the fact that Toyota's culture is driven by a different thinking process than what we as Americans are accustomed to. I'm not saying that either is necessarily right or wrong, just that they are different approaches.

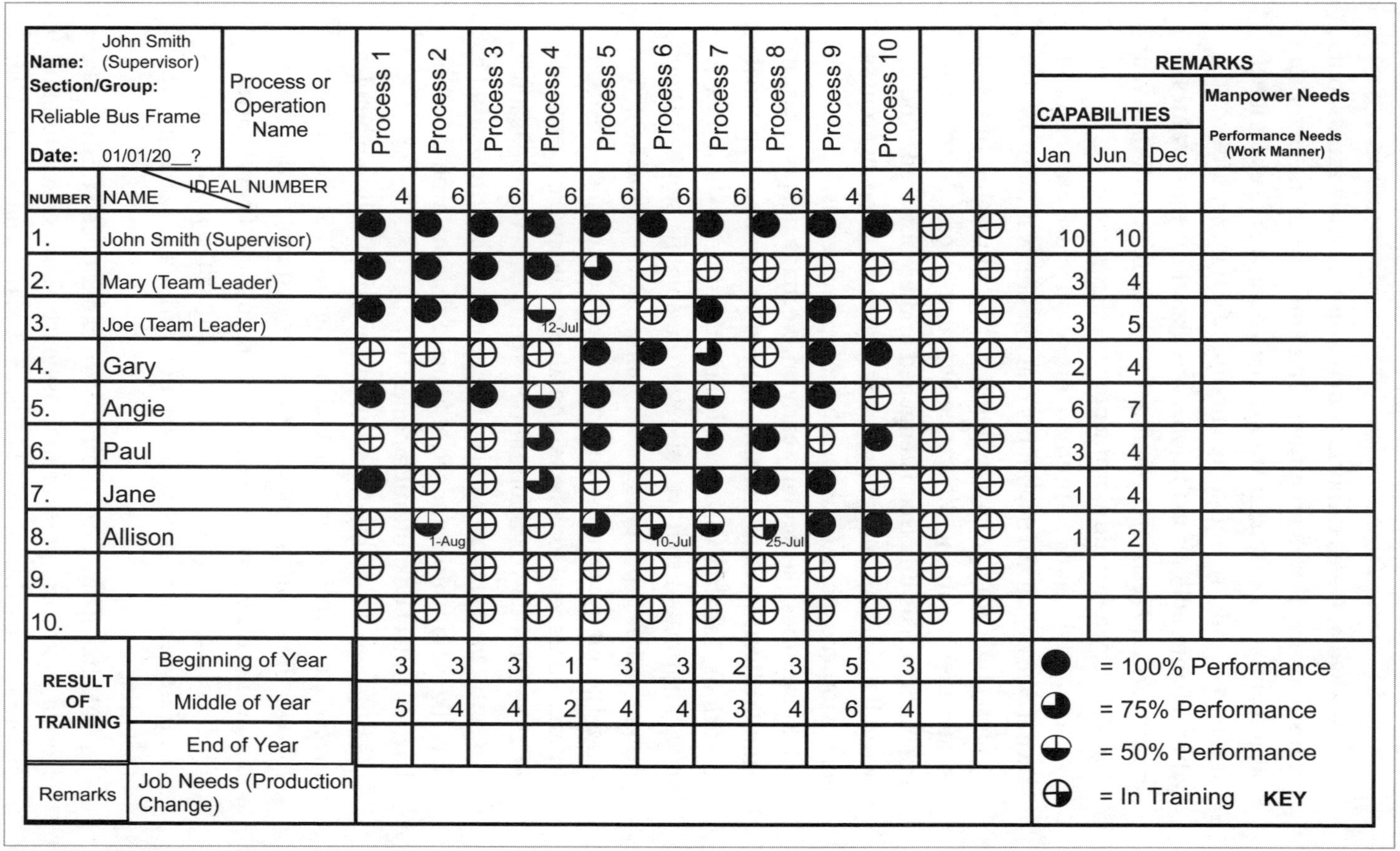

Name: John Smith (Supervisor)
Section/Group: Reliable Bus Frame
Date: 01/01/20___?

Process or Operation Name — IDEAL NUMBER

NUMBER	NAME	Process 1 (4)	Process 2 (6)	Process 3 (6)	Process 4 (6)	Process 5 (6)	Process 6 (6)	Process 7 (6)	Process 8 (6)	Process 9 (4)	Process 10 (4)	Jan	Jun	Dec
1.	John Smith (Supervisor)	●	●	●	●	●	●	●	●	●	●	10	10	
2.	Mary (Team Leader)	●	●	●	●	◑	⊕	⊕	⊕	⊕	⊕	3	4	
3.	Joe (Team Leader)	●	⊕	●	◐ (12-Jul)	⊕	⊕	●	⊕	●	⊕	3	5	
4.	Gary	⊕	⊕	⊕	⊕	●	●	⊕	●	●	●	2	4	
5.	Angie	●	●	●	●	●	●	◐	◐	⊕	●	6	7	
6.	Paul	⊕	⊕	⊕	●	⊕	⊕	⊕	●	⊕	⊕	3	4	
7.	Jane	●	◐ (1-Aug)	⊕	⊕	⊕	◐ (10-Jul)	◐	◐ (25-Jul)	●	●	1	4	
8.	Allison	⊕	⊕	⊕	⊕	⊕	⊕	⊕	⊕	⊕	⊕	1	2	
9.		⊕	⊕	⊕	⊕	⊕	⊕	⊕	⊕					
10.														

CAPABILITIES (Jan / Jun / Dec)

REMARKS: Manpower Needs · Performance Needs (Work Manner)

RESULT OF TRAINING	Process 1	Process 2	Process 3	Process 4	Process 5	Process 6	Process 7	Process 8	Process 9	Process 10
Beginning of Year	3	3	3	1	3	3	2	3	5	3
Middle of Year	5	4	4	2	4	4	3	4	6	4
End of Year										

Remarks — Job Needs (Production Change)

KEY
● = 100% Performance
◑ = 75% Performance
◐ = 50% Performance
⊕ = In Training

FIGURE 2.1 Multifunctional worker chart

At Toyota, it was important to perform as individuals, but the key element was about working and improving together as a team. It was amazing to me at a young age to experience a different culture and to see firsthand what that looked like through interactions on the job. I was absorbing those values of teamwork and respect through my daily work, and didn't even know it—it was a conditioning process.

Takahashi-san wanted to make sure we understood "what" we needed to do, but his real mission was for us to also understand "why" we were doing it. This understanding can sometimes mean the difference between a complacent team member versus one that is engaged and empowered. And as we will discuss in detail later on, it reflected a deep awareness of customer expectations and the company's goals.

Sometimes, particularly early on, we made mistakes in our standardized work, especially around sequencing. On those occasions, Takahashi-san would take the time to show us why it was important that we followed the specific steps in their proper order. If people weren't following the sequence, you would get many versions of how the work was completed, which in turn could lead to defects, and also would make it very difficult to track down abnormalities. I truly believed the leaders felt setting a standard without the proper discipline behind it was like having no standard at all, and that this would have a harmful effect on cultural morale.

This was central to the thinking of Taiichi Ohno when he placed standardization at the foundation of TPS. If everybody follows the same process in the same sequence, discrepancies, when they arise, are much easier to identify and correct. I believe that reinforcing this was Takahashi-san's mission as our trainer, and that he was very determined to see us grow in that area.

Takahashi-san and another very experienced trainer, Mr. Honda, were very present in those early days, observing and enforcing the principles of TPS to each of us as our production increased. They were also always there for us to ask questions, and I enjoyed spending time with them. I even taught Takahashi-san some English slang, and he taught us several Japanese words as well. I felt extremely lucky to get to know these wonderful trainers with so much wisdom on a one-to-one basis.

GETTING US INTO SHAPE

David Meier, former Group Leader, Toyota Motor Manufacturing Kentucky

Our Japanese trainers were rotated out every three months, and there were hundreds of them in the plant. By the time we wore them down and made them more American, the company would send in fresh recruits to smack us into shape a little bit. But they all were different.

As I learned later, most of them were team leaders with 15 to 20 years with the company. They were very skilled and knowledgeable. As well, this was their proving ground to become group leaders, so you could say that our success really was the key for their getting a promotion. So they were pretty tough on us.

Some of the trainers, like Takahashi-san, were more experienced and had been group leaders for some time. I'm pretty sure they were in line for promotion to foreman, which was the next level up for them. I found they were more people-oriented, and shared a lot of good advice on the leadership side of things.

A TOUGH LESSON

My relationships with my trainers weren't all nods and smiles. We were expected to work very hard, and our trainers could be very stern. And I, at 19, could be a bit headstrong and competitive.

We had a process, for example, for installing bolts in the backside of the instrument panel to hold the wiring harness in place. This was done with a nut runner gun, and we had to apply about 10 pounds of pressure in order to install each bolt. Because the panel was fairly wide, the standard called for the operator to install half the bolts using the right hand, and the other half using the left hand.

I was really good at this—I could blaze through it in 60 seconds, which was faster than the average. But I had learned to do it all with my right hand. My thinking was, "I can do it, leave me alone. I don't need to use my left hand. Besides, I don't feel I can control that nut runner gun with my left hand like I can with my right."

So one day, out of the blue, my trainer took me offline and asked me to leave my right hand down. "Practice this with your left hand only," he said. "Please no talking." Then he walked away without any explanation. At that moment I was a little perplexed because I really felt I was doing better than expectations just using my right hand.

Well, I was young with an occasional sarcastic flare, so I did what I was told, but I was a bit resistant the whole time. Why was he making me do this? "I was meeting all the standardized work requirements," I thought, "why pick on me like this?"

The standard, however, did say I should use both hands in the process.

Eventually, my trainer came back and asked me to explain why I had to use both hands. He waited to see how I would respond. "Do you understand why?" he asked.

"Because you said so," I retorted.

"No," he said, "the standard's there for a reason."

Then he asked me to demonstrate the process with my right hand. At one point, as I was straining over to my left, he said,

"Stop right there, and stand for 30 seconds with that pressure down." My body was in a bent position (ergonomically unsafe based on ratings), shoulder fully extended, but I hung on.

"Right now, you do this 10 times a day," he said. "You are a master. But 10 times a day is practice only." He was being a little stern with me. "But can you do this 100 times a day? Can you do this at full production at 540 times a day?"

"I am saving your shoulder," he continued. "Safety is why. Because if I do not intervene, you may hurt your shoulder. So I am saving your shoulder, and you should thank me."

"Okay, I get it—you're right," I said weakly.

"That's the first lesson," he said. "Do you know the second lesson?"

"Okay, what is it?" I asked.

"One day you will be a leader," he replied, "and you will have to deal with somebody who is resistant to change just like you."

Needless to say, I never forgot that lesson!

As TMMK progressed and became more self-sufficient with Toyota's methods, we saw less and less influence from our trainers, and today, trainers like Takahashi-san and Honda-san are few and far between. This is exactly what was supposed to happen, but I grew to miss those early days with our Japanese trainers.

Looking back, I was very young and naive at the time, and I hadn't matured to the point where I could fully appreciate the perspectives our trainers were offering. Takahashi-san had very high expectations for us all, which was sometimes intimidating for a 19-year-old, but had I known then what I know now about the priceless knowledge he and our other trainers had, I would have invested much more time asking deeper questions. Even today, I wish I could spend more time with some of my past Japanese trainers; I would have so much to ask and go see.

THE MEANING OF "NO GOOD"

David Meier, former Group Leader, Toyota Motor Manufacturing Kentucky

In one of my first job reviews, my American manager asked how my training process was going, and my trainer, who was also present, pointed his finger at me and said, "His training is no good!" I was shocked, particularly since I saw training people as one of my strengths.

But I subsequently realized that "no good" didn't mean I was a terrible trainer. "No good" meant that there were some areas where I needed to improve, which is part of life at Toyota. So there were some communication issues like this that had to get sorted out during those early days.

Some of this was about culture as well as language. One of the tenets of Asian culture is the yin and yang philosophy, where a real-life situation is considered to be a blend of two opposites. So our Japanese trainers were less likely to see our performance as black and white or "good" and "bad"—it was a combination of both. For Americans accustomed to getting either a good or bad job review, this took some getting used to.

INSTILLING TOYOTA'S VALUES

As I mentioned earlier, we were dealing with a very "raw" form of the values, principles, and methods that would eventually be documented under the titles Toyota Business Practices, the Toyota Way, and the Toyota Production System. I believe that it was necessary, due to the rapid growth of the North American organization, to codify those values for the sake of hiring and rapid training. However, it is very easy for others to study a printed document and overlook the cultural elements that are so important.

Now that the tools are out there for all to see under the "Lean" banner, people come to me and say, "OK, we've got the tools, but how do you create a culture like Toyota has?"

I tell them that's a loaded question. There are so many aspects of creating that *culture* that it's hard to give a short answer, or wave a "Harry Potter wand" and say, "Do this, and your wishes will be granted!" I wish I was that good!

As I see it, the key is understanding the difference between the *people* side of Lean and the *tool* side. The *people* side will always be the most difficult aspect—here you need the discipline to create this thing called *culture*. The *tools* are just what they are, mostly countermeasures to change some discrepancy in our process. For the *tools* to be successful, *people* must understand their involvement or the purpose behind the tools. This includes understanding exactly what to measure to ensure that any countermeasure taken is moving the needle. As I frequently remind people in our sessions, you must explain from the company perspective the "what," "how," and "why" of any change or expectation within a person's work.

Our trainers always made a point of working with us on the "what," "how," and "why" before they introduced any methods. We follow this example in our sessions so participants can begin to recognize the purpose of why they are there. When we teach our problem-solving sessions, for example, we usually spend four to five hours on the cultural aspects before we even begin to talk about some of the practical steps.

To help people visualize what's involved on the culture side, we use a model that we call the culture chain, which is illustrated in Figure 2.2. This was adapted from a quotation from the Indian political leader and philosopher Mahatma Gandhi, which was introduced to me by Mike Hoseus.

We have found that the culture chain is a very effective way of showing how we internalize the values and principles that we live with every day. Let's look at how this thinking applies to a continuous improvement culture.

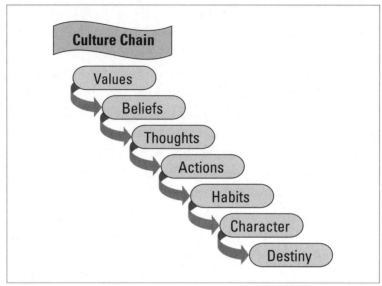

FIGURE 2.2 Culture chain

Values or principles are the starting point. These are the guiding beacons that we can relate to specific tangible actions in our daily activities that bring to life the values. For example, Toyota has a set of values called the Toyota Way. They are:

- Go to See
- Teamwork
- Challenge
- Continuous Improvement
- Respect for People

Each value supports tangible actions I can apply or transmit to others within my daily work.

The next aspect is *beliefs*. Do the people *believe* in what the company is trying to accomplish through its values or principles? Do people respect their leaders? Do people believe that the company has their best interest at heart? Do people come to work with the best interest of the company at heart? (These are, by the way, good questions to ask of people within your organization to get a barometer check on the morale level.) This is often referred to as mutual trust and respect. These are all aspects of the belief system within a culture.

While I was at Toyota I could honestly say that I believed in what the company was trying to accomplish each day through our rigid standard work. It meant something, and I had a real bond with the product I was creating. I could see it in the Camry I was driving, and would pull up at stop lights and think, "My initials are inside that instrument panel."

Our leaders tried very hard to "live the values" through their work each day—they taught us that our beliefs were essential to the culture we were creating. Without it, Lean, or whatever you want to call it, can only be a program or a "flavor of the month."

In order for a belief to take hold for the individual or leader, it must become part of their daily *thoughts* when they walk in the door each day. If that belief becomes an intrinsic thought, then it's more likely to lead to *action(s)* that align with the company values and principles. It is the responsibility of leaders to develop their people in these areas, and this places an enormous amount on their shoulders. It's not possible to "order" a person to adopt a way of thinking—this can only be taught using the servant leader model, where leaders teach by example and always stay "one step ahead" of their learners with an "I work for you" mentality. This is difficult for people accustomed to the traditional top-down hierarchical mindset, which in turn is why successful implementation of Lean culture is so rare.

So all eyes are on the leaders, who can make or break the Lean culture very easily. This is why when I train at various companies I ask for their leadership to be trained first if possible.

Once *values, beliefs, thoughts,* and *actions* have been established, the mental process starts to become a *habit*. This is what we arrived at when we worked for TMMK, and this is where the culture becomes "atmospheric." Here, it is no longer a matter of choice or convenience—it's part of your everyday life.

In essence this became the *character* of our workforce— what we all accepted as the way we did business. We didn't call it anything, but there was never any doubt that we were accountable for maintaining that discipline, which, once again, is very difficult when you approach your work with a traditional mindset.

Once your workforce has built that character, then it's the *destiny* of the company to become a market leader and a place of choice for employment. I am willing to state categorically that if you create the kind of culture that this culture chain defines, you will get the kind of results that can only come from solid processes and efficient sharing of knowledge throughout the organization. This is where we make our biggest departure from traditional management. Most companies rely on the "manage by the number" or results only, forgetting the people along the way. We are saying the opposite—start with your people first.

The following quote appears in the Toyota Way values book:

> *"People are the most important asset of Toyota and the determinant of the rise or fall of Toyota"*
>
> —EIJI TOYODA, former CEO and Chairman of Toyota

So please focus on the people side and ask yourself: "Where am I in this 'culture chain' of thinking?" "Where are my gaps?" and "How do I begin to close them?"

TO IMPROVE, YOU MUST HAVE STANDARDS

It was within this deep context of culture and individual thinking that the idea of maintaining and improving standards was presented to us. If we all understand the "why" behind standards and truly "own" the processes, we don't have to be told what to do by our leaders, and they can spend their time developing us so that we get even better at improving the processes and the standards. So this is all part of a virtuous circle.

In a broader sense, this deep everyday awareness of the "why" behind the standards helps create an environment where we manage our processes instead of having them manage us.

In the beginning phases of TMMK, a lot of the production areas were still being constructed. We were, at times, taping off shadow images of where items of equipment would be placed before they arrived from Japan.

Consequently, our standards at the beginning were works in progress. This is another unique aspect of our experience— you really get to understand what standards are about when you are involved in creating them side by side with people who have a deep understanding of them.

The standards initially grew out of a large-scale planning process. Ernie spent a month in Japan preparing for this right after he was hired as a team leader. While there he spent time at the Tsutsumi plant, which was the model we used as the starting point for many of our processes. Here, he participated in visualization exercises, learning some of the layouts and standardized work for the Powertrain area.

However, this wasn't about giving TMMK's leaders something to copy; the purpose was to gain a deep understanding of the complexity of building an axle for a Toyota Camry. Once Ernie returned, he and his trainer Mr. Shoichi Ikoma (Ikoma-san), along with his group leader and team members, developed a high-level process outline of what the standards would look like once everything arrived.

Many businesses use flow charts and process outlines, but with the Toyota Production System, all our processes are built on a single principle. Here, we are designing processes so that *we can build a car in the time that the customer demands.*

To simplify, let's say that a customer walks in the door on average once per minute and asks for a new car. This means that we have to design our processes so that we can create a new car every 60 seconds.

The term we used for that 60 seconds is *takt* time, which is based on a German word that means "measure time." When we began production in September 1988 at TMMK, our *takt* time was somewhere around 60 seconds.

What this means, if you think about it, is that every production task must be repeated, on average, every 60 seconds. Of course, there were many variations on this, but the main idea is that we were dealing with tasks that took place in short increments of time, and we used written documents to standardize each task so that our *takt* time could be met consistently.

This took meticulous planning. During TMMK's start-up, process design began at the highest levels and progressed to the more specific. For example, the planners would pencil out the layout of equipment and begin to discuss the work-flow path necessary to operate the process so that it would consistently meet the eventual *takt* time. Once the layout and work flow were penciled out, they started to look at the time it would take to complete the work at each station.

We would then get involved in creating or revising the standards for our own area. This involved documenting in more detail the standardized work tasks, creating job breakdown sheets for job instruction training, work combination tables to embed equipment time in, and multifunctional worker charts for a training status visual of each person as we evolved.

Figure 2.3 shows an example of a "vintage" work standard from about 1987, back in the days when standards were often handwritten. There was typically a list of subtasks in the left column, often clarified with illustrations on the right. Standards were very precise, specifying which tool and which hand to use, and of course, any safety requirements.

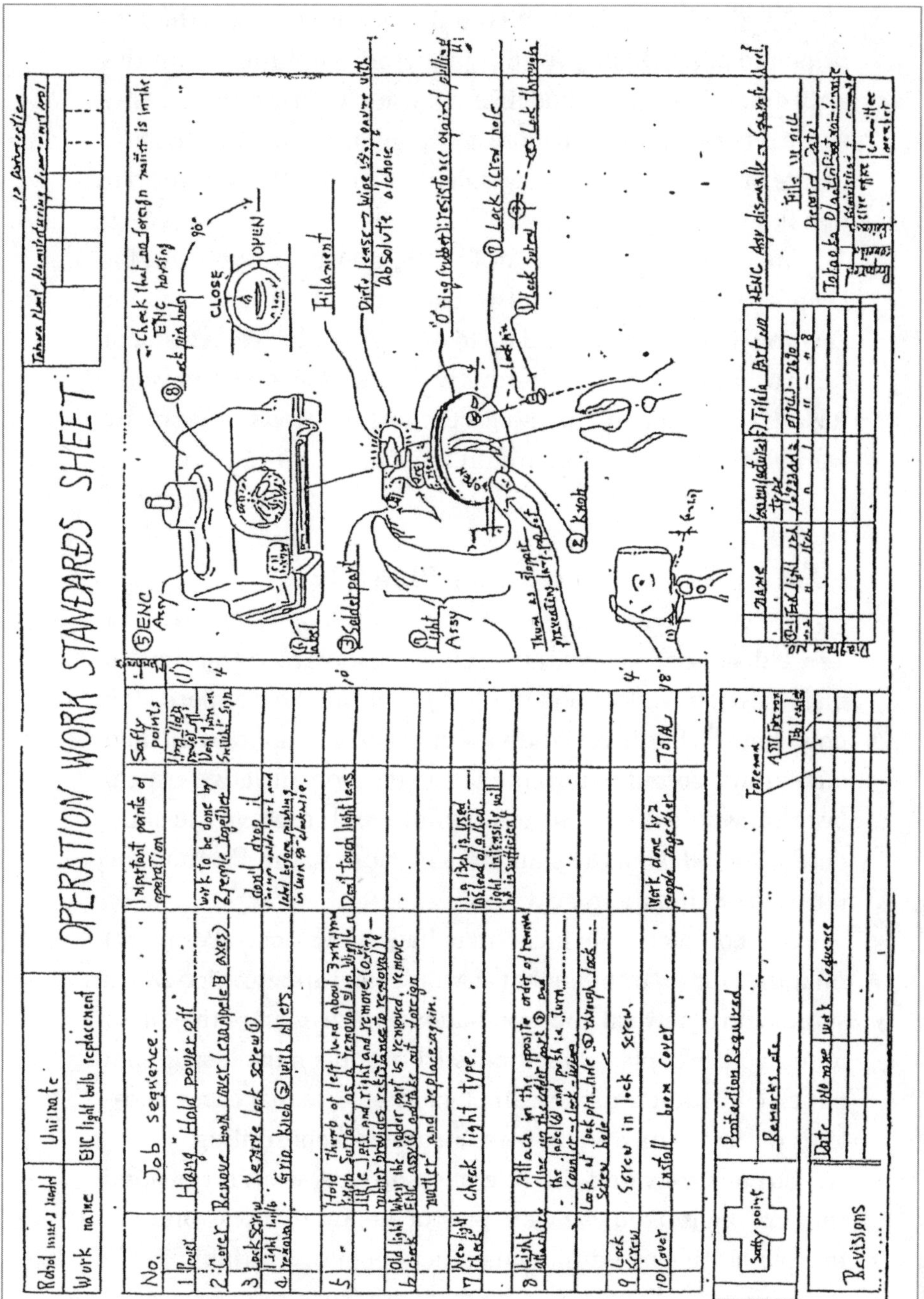

FIGURE 2.3 Vintage work standard

This thinking behind the standards was central to the TPS principle of producing in the right amount of time, with the right amount of people and inventory, and with minimal waste. As we received more and more equipment, we adjusted the fine points of the layout, work, people, and material and information flow.

Once production began at TMMK, we were responsible for keeping these standards posted at our workstations, and for keeping them readable and up to date. We didn't even think of them as something special—this was just how we did our work. It wasn't until later on in my career that I realized that so many workplaces have no standards at all.

BEYOND COMPLIANCE

As we discussed earlier, our trainers always took the time to make sure we understood the "why" behind the standard. The point here is that Toyota didn't want us to put our brain on hold and blindly comply—it wanted us to develop an active critical eye that would enable us to maintain and improve the standards. We followed the standards because we understood the purpose behind them.

Our connection to customers had many facets. We might imagine, for example, what it would feel like to discover a scratch on a new car that you had just driven out of the lot, or to see a piece of plastic molding sticking out on the instrument panel. Our standards were in place to ensure that these problems didn't occur, and that our customers kept smiling.

But our role, and the role of standards, went far beyond that. As mentioned, we were part of a team that was producing cars at the speed that customers demanded them. Every improvement allowed us to do that with fewer resources, even though the needle moved in very small increments. As we will see in Part 2, the Toyota culture was not so much about home runs achieved by a few people, but about many, many base hits achieved by all of us. So the "why" behind a given standard might have been that it had proven to be the fastest way to accomplish a task, even if it didn't appear that way on the surface.

Another important "why" in standards was safety, and this was considered an absolute. Safety was embedded into every standard and carefully considered whenever a standard was reviewed or revised. So if there was a faster way that would cause strain on the worker, that was never an option.

We'll look more deeply at the "why" of standards in Part 2.

JUST DOING OUR JOBS

David Meier, former Group Leader, Toyota Motor Manufacturing Kentucky

I think we were experiencing something new and exciting, and we knew that the world was watching. We got the Gold Plant Award for Quality after only about three years, and this was unheard-of. How does this start-up plant with all these folks who had no experience go from zero to the top in such a short period of time?

So we were doing things that had never been done before— we had the fastest ramp-up, and were setting all kinds of records, but we didn't necessarily think about that every day. We were just doing what we needed to do.

DEALING WITH ABNORMALITIES

No matter what we did at TMMK, standards were always in the forefront of our thinking. When something didn't appear to be right, we were conditioned to immediately ask ourselves what the standard was. When Takahashi-san criticized me for engaging in the unsafe practice of using my right hand only, he would have instantly considered these three possibilities:

1. There was no standard that accounted for the situation.
2. The standard existed, but was not being followed.
3. The standard was outdated or incorrect.

In my case, the standard existed, but I was not following it because I felt that I was making my objectives doing it "my way." It was my duty to either follow the standard or make a case for changing it.

If there was no standard, or if the standard was incorrect, there was no "standards officer" who would eventually come along and correct the situation. At Toyota, this was up to us, and we often did it on the spot.

If some problem was preventing us from completing our work successfully according to standard, our first step was to pull the *andon*, a cord above the workstation that activates a warning light and/or audio alarm. This alerted our team leader or group leader to provide support. If the problem couldn't be resolved within an allowable time buffer, our leader would pull the *andon* again, shutting down the entire line.

While a line stoppage is considered an extreme measure in traditional manufacturing, it occurred frequently at Toyota. This practice of not waiting to fix problems, called *jidoka*, is one of the foundations of Toyota's approach.

THE IMPORTANCE OF IDENTIFYING PROBLEMS

Mike Hoseus, former Assistant General Manager of Operations and HR at Toyota Motor Manufacturing Kentucky and Executive Director, The Center for Quality People and Organizations.

When I did my initial training in Japan, one of the big "aha" moments for me was discovering the power of the *andon*. In most organizations, problem identification is an even bigger issue than problem solving. But what I discovered early on was the social aspect. Raising your hand when there's a problem doesn't mean that this is a problem with you; it means that you have a problem. And the *andon* was pulled for even very small deviations from the standard, so *andon* pulls were very frequent. So what I could see is that in Japan, they didn't have fewer problems in their factories. They identified them, corrected then, and learned from them. That was the difference.

However, the workaround mentality is hard to shed sometimes. My group had a new supplier for plastic fender liners, and the holes weren't lining up with the body. So I had a guy sweating away, bending the fender liners so they would fit, and I thanked him for his hard work and went on about my work. Not much later, my trainer called me back over to his area and asked, "What is he doing?"

"Oh, I already thanked him, because he's working his tail off getting those liners to fit, isn't he?" I said.

"No, no, this is no good," he said.

"Why? He's working hard," I said.

"Mike-san, you must teach him to do his job," he said.

"I thought he's doing his job," I said.

"No. If he can't do standardized work, his job is to pull the *andon* to identify the problem," he said. "So please teach him

> to do his job so that you can do your job, which is to solve the problem."
>
> "Okay," I said. I had lots of "aha" moments like that where I had to learn a new way of thinking.

FUNDAMENTALS OF IMPROVEMENT

As many readers will be aware, improvements at Toyota were conducted scientifically based on the classic Plan, Do, Check, Act (PDCA) paradigm. However, our first exposure to this thinking was through a variant called SDCA, an acronym for Standardize, Do, Check, Act.

This approach reflected Taiichi Ohno's observation that you can't have improvement without standards. In other words, you have to fully understand how standards are supposed to work before you can contemplate revising one.

Learning to develop and revise standards was therefore one of the most foundational learnings from my trainers. I remember when Takahashi-san first introduced us to the SDCA process using a flipchart. He drew a diagram that looked like Figure 2.4.

When using SDCA, you "Standardize" first, determining the best known standard for meeting the internal and external customer needs. Once you determine the correct standard, you continue the process by putting it into place with the "Do" phase and "Check" the effectiveness of your change based on the performance measures before and after the change. When you have determined that it's meeting the expectation, then the "Act" stage is used to make it the new documented policy or procedure and share it with other affected areas. This becomes the benchmark for improvement.

Speaking practically, applying the SDCA process before we start changing our processes reduces the amount of

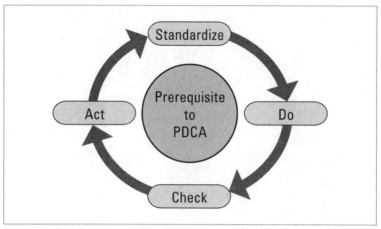

FIGURE 2.4 SDCA: Standardize, Do, Check, Act

discrepancies or rework we have each day because our standards aren't as clear and concise as they should be. I can't begin to count the amount of waste that hemorrhages out the door of companies every minute because standardization is weak or poorly thought out, forcing people to "wing it."

CHANGING THE PROCESS

Once we had determined through SDCA that the cause of a particular problem could not be resolved by fixing the standard, we could start to work directly on the process itself. Here, we turned to the classic version of PDCA that many are familiar with.

The Plan, Do, Check, Act (PDCA) paradigm, popularized in the latter half of the twentieth century by W. Edwards Deming, is a simple method for correcting deviations that has become the cornerstone of continuous improvement. PDCA is widely used in organizations, but it is usually employed as a tool, as opposed to a way of thinking.

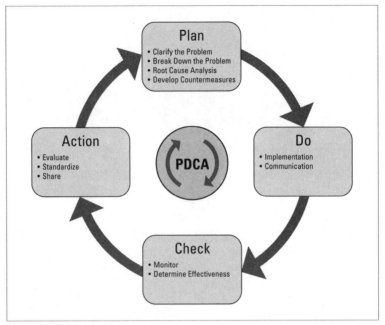

FIGURE 2.5 PDCA: Plan, Do, Check, Act

At TMMK, PDCA was really embedded in our thinking. We knew, for example, that when we started to communicate with our trainers about a problem, the lens for examining it would be PDCA, and this thinking would be applied very rigorously.

With PDCA, we were learning how to build cars that would create even bigger smiles from customers than models in the previous year had. Ian Bradbury, a board member of the W. Edwards Deming Institute, aptly described PDCA as "a learning cycle in which you are trying to build both knowledge of customer value and knowledge of the means of production for customer value simultaneously."

When used correctly, PDCA is a systematic or scientific way of thinking where we ask Socratic questions in a designed sequence, allowing problems to be effectively and efficiently solved. If you bypass the process and jump over crucial steps, then the process may be compromised and your results could be skewed—or your success might just be due to luck. Consequently, PDCA has many built-in mechanisms that keep the owner in check. I often say if the process talks to you and you listen, then it's working.

As leaders, we were committed to be developing people so that this thinking became intrinsic and part of the everyday business practice. To promote this, Toyota developed the eight-step problem-solving process that later became known as Toyota Business Practices (TBP). We will discuss this in detail in Part 2.

BRINGING PEOPLE TOGETHER TO SOLVE PROBLEMS

My first intensive involvement with PDCA took place during my participation in Quality Circles. The practice was modeled on the Quality Circle movement in Japan, where autonomous groups of workers, typically 7 to 10 workers, meet regularly outside of production hours to identify, define, and solve problems in the workplace. These Quality Circle (QC) activities often led to creating new standardized work together with the rest of the team.

I signed up for one of the first Quality Circles in Plastics and was part of that inaugural process. Several of our successful projects helped my immediate Instrument Panels group.

The QC format was very similar to PDCA, but the company tracked and monitored our progress as we completed each step of the process. You had to share ideas, follow PDCA, and then create new standard work with the team leaders if the ideas were validated through experimentation. This allowed for communication of our problem to others and gave us opportunities to involve our stakeholders or anyone that may have touched the problem that needed to understand if a process changed. This allowed me to practice in a very open-formatted environment—not only to hone my problem-solving skills, but to learn personalities and dynamics of people a lot better.

Successful projects, however, were not the primary purpose of Quality Circles—the number one priority was developing people. Therefore, it was a really good program for learning how to listen to others, document the work, and practice the thinking under the Toyota Production System, and I credit much of my development to those formative activities.

Quality Circles were also, as it turned out, my "boot camp" for progressing to a leadership role. After working through several activities, I decided to enroll in the class to become a Quality Circle leader. This would challenge me at an entirely different level: I wasn't responsible just for myself, but now for a team. This meant I had to not only guide others as a fellow team member, but coach problem solving and foster ideas. Little did I know I was developing myself for the next level. All this took place across a three-year span, but slowly I was creating base hits preparing myself for a home run one day.

There are, however, some aspects of leadership that nobody can prepare for, as you will see in the next chapter.

3

Becoming a Leader

■ ■ ■

Growing up, I was not what people would call a natural born leader. I never ran for student council, and even though I was on many sports teams, I never had the confidence to be a team captain. I was also terrified of speaking out in class and would often sit silently while other more gregarious students asked questions and made comments.

At TMMK, however, there was something in the atmosphere that made me think, "I could be a leader here one day." I began to get a sense of that in the evaluation process that led to my getting hired, and I felt it very strongly on my first day as an employee, when I received my red Team Toyota T-shirt. For reasons I didn't yet understand, I intuitively felt "at home" at TMMK.

Consequently, I resolved to do whatever it would take to become a leader almost from day one. My leaders and trainers welcomed my enthusiasm and challenged me to develop my leadership potential. Their belief in me helped me believe in myself, and I will always be deeply grateful for that.

My formal preparation to be a leader began in 1990 when I got approval to begin prepromotion team leader training courses. This led to a series of prerequisite courses on a variety of subjects. Some of the courses were quite specific to our environment, including areas like problem solving (this covered the PDCA/A3 approach in detail) and job instruction assessment. Others, such as listening skills and meeting facilitation, were more general, although TMMK's approach to these subjects was quite unique.

What really stood out in these courses was the emphasis on the thinking behind the concepts. Methods were just one aspect—the nuances of how people interacted with them were the essential enablers that made them work. I found the coursework very engaging. Our instructors spent a lot of time making sure we understood the "why" behind the concepts, and they expected us to think. They also understood that people have different learning styles and adapted their training accordingly. I only wish there had been the opportunity for this kind of learning when I was in school!

At the same time, the courses were extremely demanding, and classes were held before or after our shifts, and sometimes on weekends. Our instructors expected us to really push ourselves even when we were very tired, and I often called upon my family work gene to keep me motivated.

The hard work paid off when, at age 21, I was promoted to a team leader position in Plastics.

"NEVER BE COMFORTABLE!"

I can vividly remember the moment when my trainer presented me with my hat that identified me as a team leader—blue with a brown strip. "Tracey-san, always be uncomfortable," he said. I wasn't sure exactly what he meant by this, but I was very excited about being entrusted to set an example for a team of five or six people, and to coach and support them to the best of my abilities. And I was very proud to wear the hat.

Over time, I learned that "uncomfortable" meant embracing challenges rather than shying away from them. It meant avoiding complacency at all costs. And it meant avoiding the "telling-selling-convincing" trap that leaders often fall into and following the much more demanding "engage-involve-empower" example that my leaders and trainers so aptly set.

As mentioned earlier, I was not comfortable speaking in front of groups, even of only three or four. People could actually hear a tremor in my voice when I spoke. Clearly, it would have been difficult for me to become a leader in a lot of companies.

TMMK, it turned out, saw my leadership potential in a very different light—the trainers saw that I was always asking "why," listening, and respecting people, and had a particular passion for helping others "see light bulbs." These were the qualities that they felt were most important. And when it came to competencies outside of my comfort zone, they had confidence that I would develop them, even though there were times when I wasn't too sure myself. And as we'll see later, they gave me a big push when I least expected it.

Team leaders, technically speaking, are hourly workers with no formal management authority who provide mentorship, support, and oversight for their group. Team leaders spend the majority of their time at or near the process supporting the team when discrepancies occur. For matters involving corrective action or performance issues, team leaders must defer to their group leader.

The team leader is also the immediate "go to" person if a problem comes up that a team member can't resolve on the spot. If somebody pulls the *andon*, the team leader is the first responder. It was also my responsibility to jump into the line if a team member was falling behind or had arrived late. (Remember how I had to change my habits when I first started at Toyota?)

As well, I kept a watchful eye for deviations from standard work and pointed these out to people. Safety was the top priority, and I was expected to intervene if that was ever in doubt.

The same applied if quality standards weren't being met. And again, if an issue with a team member persisted, I reported that to my group leader.

During this period, I continued to learn very rapidly, and my leaders, far from ignoring me, challenged me to develop my skills further. This included more courses, which at this point in my development pertained to leading Quality Circles. As was common practice at TMMK, Quality Circles became my "boot camp" for practicing and improving my leadership skills. It was here that I began to extend my comfort zone around interacting with people, and to make inroads on conquering my fear of speaking in front of groups.

The experience also helped me gain a deeper understanding of some of the thinking behind Toyota's vision of leadership. For example, the Japanese word *nemawashi* was used quite often in our environment, and it is usually expressed in English as gaining consensus or getting proper buy-in. At a high level this is correct, but the real meaning was a little more subtle than that. I can remember once my trainer describing *nemawashi* as "prepping the soil" to plant a tree. When he noticed my puzzled look, he asked me to think about what is necessary for that to take place and for the tree to flourish.

After I had articulated that process step by step, he asked me to imagine that the tree was an idea. How can we cultivate ideas on a daily basis and prepare them for sharing and applying among the team? As leaders we must always be *prepping the soil*, not only for an individual but for the team and how that cascades upward to the company. It's an important challenge everyone must embrace.

As mentioned, my leaders constantly looked for opportunities for me to step outside of my comfort zone, which led to an unforgettable experience for me. Our group had completed a project that involved rebalancing the workforce so people could be utilized in different areas that needed manpower. The purpose was to avoid hiring more additional people than was absolutely necessary—a key priority since lifetime employment is a core value for Toyota. The project was very exciting because it allowed us to simulate ideas on the line in real time without compromising lead time or quality.

To track our progress, we used closely monitored items like excessive walking, potential wait time, machine time, setup time, delay work (*andon* pull), and the standardized work steps involved. Over a two-week period, we continued to look for improvements so we could trial, measure, and modify the current standards to meet the new expectations. Seeing the process come to life in this fashion was very exciting, and I became passionate about the project.

At the time, manpower rebalancing was a big issue throughout the plant, and after we had successfully changed our standards to adjust for some of the new improvements, it then became our duty to "share the wisdom" with other departments. Soon, a formal presentation was arranged, and it turned out that Shoichiro Toyoda was going to be present. Now, having the chairman of the Toyota Motor Corporation, not to mention a member of the iconic Toyoda family, at our *gemba* was not something that happened every day, so our area was buzzing with excitement.

Then, to my surprise, I was asked if I would be willing to deliver a portion of the presentation that involved the area where I was team leader. Initially, I was terrified. I had never done anything like this before—I'd never actually had to speak with a microphone. "Are you serious?" I said, "You want me to speak in front of Mr. Shoichiro Toyoda and all the high-level leaders at TMMK? What if I mess up? What if I get too nervous?"

But as the day approached, I realized that this wasn't just about sharing what we had learned in the *kaizen*—my trainers saw this as a developmental opportunity for me. Yes, I was nervous when I presented (Figure 3.1), but I somehow powered through because I was passionate about my role and the activities we had completed as a team. This was a moment for me where I was uncomfortable, yet learning so much at the same time.

FIGURE 3.1 Formal presentation with Shoichiro Toyoda

My trainer was right; it was perfectly fine to be in the uncomfortable zone. Actually, we all should stay in it! Over time, my leaders and trainers helped me shed my introverted shell to the point where I became a trainer. I will always be thankful I was asked to be part of this activity, and that it led me to meet a member of the iconic Toyoda family.

COMFORT ZONES

Tanya Doyle, Lean Culture Coach

Being outside your comfort zone is the only way you can grow—you actually have to learn. For us Lean people, that's what it's all about. We're constantly solving problems and setting new goals and target conditions for improvement. That's part of how we live, and that's why we don't fit in normal businesses where people sit in their siloed offices and send e-mails to each other.

I continued to take courses and practice my leadership skills during the years I served in the team leader role. For two of those, I served on the pilot team—a special team responsible for integrating production changes on the line preparing for the next model launch. Pilot teams were in their infancy at that point, so this was one of those priceless situations where our leaders were learning along with us. Over my time there I witnessed a model changeover going from a few days down to minutes. It was amazing to see and be part of that type of running model change, and a great lesson in practicing all the facets of PDCA.

I transferred to the headliner group in 1994, and a year later, after serving a total of five years in the team leader role, I was promoted to the position of group leader for that group.

LEADING AND LEARNING

My trainer came to my area shortly after my promotion and asked me, "Tracey-san, are you ready to be a leader?" Then, to make sure I understood the implications of this, he continued, "Please understand that as a leader, you must now spend 50 percent of your time developing your people."

Becoming group leader meant a change from hourly to salaried employee, and this came with significant responsibility. From here on I would be ultimately judged on the long-term success of my team members. This servant leadership role is the cornerstone of Toyota's unique approach to management. For group leaders, having the discipline to complete our considerable day-to-day management duties efficiently was only the starting point—the real test was how, in the remaining 50 percent of our time, we served the learning needs of our people.

In my new role, I was responsible for five team leaders and an entire group of approximately 30 people. I was now directly responsible for their attendance, personnel file, daily labor management, rotational cross-training, strategy cascading of the KPIs (key performance indicators), visualization, and most important, maintaining standard work. I think the moment they offered me the position and handed me the group leader hat with the blue stripe I knew I would have to once again raise the bar on myself.

I found it encouraging to reflect on the following words from Sakichi Toyoda: *"I have experienced many twists and turns in my life; many battles hard fought and skirmishes half won. For the most part, I have seen more failures than successes."*

This was always humbling to me, and it was also comforting to know that failure is something that even great leaders must confront. I reflected on this often in my early months as a group leader, where my trainers would sometimes let me go down a rabbit hole and fail just to bring a learning point to the forefront.

Furthermore, I took on the group leader responsibility with great pride. Here I was, at age 26, responsible for creating a safe workplace where 30 people could find the satisfaction of sharing their talents and developing their skill sets in order to give our customers the best cars that we could make. Today I'm still proud to know that my initials and the initials of the people I helped develop are still a part of over a million cars on the road.

While many aspects of the group leader role can only be learned by experience, the responsibilities are very clearly defined. In your area, you are responsible for all materials, equipment, and people being in in their proper place and condition at the beginning of a shift and at the end of a shift.

You begin each day by leading the daily stand-up meeting with your team members. Here, you advise people of targets, quality and safety alerts, staffing changes, special recognition of team members, cross-training plans, and relevant company information.

All day long, you keep a watchful eye on numerous indicators that might impact safety, quality, delivery, or cost, knowing that any abnormality that arises during the shift is your responsibility. And on top of that, you have to keep your people informed, address any personnel issues that arise, and act on your team members' behalf to remove any barriers that might be in their way.

Throughout the day, I spent most of my time at the *gemba*, checking all the visual management indicators, updating charts, and simply observing the work of my team at their specific work process. I was always asking myself as well as my team, how can we identify and reduce waste, or shave off a few seconds here or there (this could be minutes, hours, or days in other industries) to improve our delivery time while maintaining quality and not causing overwork or safety problems?

Often I would talk with workers by asking questions. How did they feel the work was going? Did they see any ways we could do things better? What did they need from me to be successful? And finally, how were things going for them outside of their working life? Toyota truly cares for employees, and as their leader, I was Toyota's representative.

This role, of course, was radically different from traditional managers who work in offices and only interact with their people to deal with a crisis, announce targets, reinforce rules and policies, or assign blame when things go wrong.

FINDING TIME FOR LEADING AND LEARNING

Fran Vescio, Project Manager, Education Sector

While struggling through a crazy week of meetings and a million other things that I needed to accomplish—oh, and trying to find time to lead—I stumbled upon this quote.

"Minds are like parachutes; they work best when open."

—**Thomas Dewar,** Scottish businessman

> It reminded me of something that Tracey taught us about how dangerous it is to be firefighting all the time and not making time to be a good servant leader.
>
> If you recall, being a servant leader *is not* having all the answers, but it *is* about asking all the right questions, helping your team members and coworkers (and you) understand the situation and formulate the best solutions, and creating leading and learning lessons along the way. If we fail to do this, we will not have open parachutes. Instead, we will continue to fight fires, diminishing value and morale of ourselves and those around us.

Needless to say, balancing the daily tasks required of a group leader with the responsibility of developing my people was very challenging. I had become quite comfortable at assisting team members in my five years as a team leader, so it was natural for me to go on the line and help a team leader with a process problem, or even help adjust equipment parameters. Instead, I had to learn how to coach people so that they'd become less dependent on my help.

My first failure was that I didn't push myself hard enough out of my comfort zone of pleasing people rather than developing them. I soon discovered that I had to be a bit of a chameleon, adjusting to the different learning styles of my team members. For example, some people need more details or deeper explanations as to why something is important, and some may be easily overwhelmed by too much information.

This got more difficult when groups of people were involved. At TMMK, the environment is changing all the time, and there has to be excellent ongoing communication between people in research, design, engineering, and maintenance. And when you consider that decisions are made by consensus, communication had to be thorough, timely, and consistent.

Managing changes in a process could therefore be quite complex. When we did pilots, for example, we sometimes had to make temporary adjustments so that we could run trials in an area without disrupting regular production, making sure that all equipment parameters would revert to the original standard once the pilot was completed. Some changes were easily integrated into the line, but others required discussions so that workers could see the feasibility of our initial hypotheses and gain an understanding of the reasoning behind the changes.

Of course, I had failures along the way. I can remember discussions that were frustrating for both sides because I didn't engage a person properly, or didn't take the time to effectively explain the purpose behind the changes. Sometimes when you are close to something and understand all the nuances, you assume that others have that same level of understanding. I've often said knowledge and experience can be viewed as a "blessing or a curse."

I was also on a strict timeline with limited equipment usage, so I sometimes felt that bypassing discussions was the easiest path for me. As a result, I got some team member resistance to a few of the ideas I introduced because team members perceived that the change would create more work, or make the work more difficult.

A subtle point here is something we called *mental burden*, which we defined as the number of decisions a person would have to make in his or her 60-second *takt* time. If there are more than 8 to 10 decisions in a process (this could vary depending on the industry), it can create an avenue for discrepancies. So I had to work closely with the team members doing the work and carefully go through all the decision points in their job.

The big lesson in all of this is how essential trust is when it comes to getting things done in a continuous improvement environment. You really need to start with the understanding that without people's buy-in, the success rate for implementation can be lowered significantly. It was important, therefore, for me to constantly communicate to my team members that I understood their work, and how changes would affect them.

I think of trust as a blank sheet of paper. If I take that paper and wrinkle it up in a ball and then do my best to smooth it out, it will never quite be the way it was. I might try different methods like a steam iron, but there will still be some residue of creases in the paper. I think trust is like that—if there is not a strong culture of mutual trust and respect right from the start, people will develop creases that they carry with them.

What I gradually realized was that I was responsible for the complete work environment that my team members experienced every day. At TMMK, we didn't want an environment that had a feeling of drudgery to it, but rather a place where people felt empowered and motivated to challenge themselves and work with the team to test new ideas for making their work more efficient and more effective.

This meant that as a leader, I had to lead by example and spend my days challenging myself openly. Our trainers often referred to that as *leading and learning simultaneously*. This practice allowed us to learn but at the same time coach.

"How is it possible to lead and learn at the same time?" one might ask. "Isn't it necessary for us to have the answers first?" Here's how I like to phrase my answer: Lead not from a position of power, but from an empowering position.

This means that when facing an uncertain situation, you might have to say to a team member, "I don't know," and that is OK. You can then say, "Let's go see and find out together and learn." To many that might be uncomfortable at first because we have been conditioned as humans to think that the boss always has the answers. If the boss doesn't know, then he or she shouldn't be the boss, correct?

It turns out that there is some mythology here. Managers fear that if they admit that they don't know, then their workers will lose respect for them. But it is obvious to workers that managers can't possibly know everything, and they respect those who have the confidence to lead without pretending to have all the answers. I've seen ample proof of that at TMMK, and in companies that truly "get it" when it comes to continuous improvement culture.

AVOIDING BIG COMPANY DISEASE

David Meier, former Group Leader,
Toyota Motor Manufacturing Kentucky

The joke at Toyota was that if you achieve a great result, you get about two seconds of glory where they say, "Okay, nice job. But now let me ask you a million questions about what you did." And for me, initially, that was hard, that was difficult because I was thinking, "Well they're asking me all these questions. I must have done something wrong." So I'd try to anticipate that, and give them answers to every question I could think of before they asked it. But that didn't work, because they never ran out of questions.

So here we were, hitting all kinds of targets and getting accolades from outside, but internally, they were saying, "That's great, but we have to keep going." I soon learned that their greatest fear was something they called "big company disease," which is really apathy. The Toyota guys were concerned that we would start thinking, "We're awesome, we're number one, let's sit back." They told us the Tortoise and the Hare story a million times.

So management worked very hard to counter that. At every management-type meeting that we had with the people from Japan, they were always very reluctant to acknowledge that at some point in the future we were going to pass Ford or GM or something and be "number one." I mean, they really didn't want to be number one, honestly.

TOYOTA AND BEYOND

After 10 years of working in production, I faced a very tough decision. As group leader, I was working second shift, which is 5:15 p.m. until 2:00 a.m., while Ernie, who was two levels above me in management, was on a regular day shift. That might have been all right if we were hourly workers, but as management, we both spent a lot of time outside of our regular shifts, including weekends. As a result, we hardly ever saw each other.

At the same time, I was experiencing a growing desire to help people learn the lessons my trainers had passed on to me. I had "lived" the deeper style of learning that they had introduced me to, and thoroughly believed in it. I wondered how I could pursue this path further.

The ideal situation for me personally would have been to move into human resources training and development. However, Ernie's group was a part of the overall Human Resources department, and Toyota, understandably, had strict guidelines around people transferring to a department where their spouse was already a full-time employee. Making that change, therefore, would have been difficult.

So Ernie and I decided that the best option was to give up my position and pursue a career as a contractor/consultant. Here, I could share the wisdom and knowledge I had gathered over the years and become a trainer under a potentially different context.

It wasn't clear to me at the time how this might play out. I suspected that as TMMK continued to wean itself from Japanese trainers, there might be opportunities within the Toyota organization. As well, Toyota was expanding rapidly, and it turned out that many job applicants were not able to meet the hiring criteria that Toyota had set. Some of them resorted to phoning TMMK Human Resources and asking, "Where can I learn this stuff?" Apparently, many of the basic skills that Toyota looked for in the hiring process weren't being taught anywhere.

In response to this, and after many discussions with all parties, Toyota began a partnership with the Scott County school system in Georgetown to experiment with bringing some of these concepts into our local schools. It began with some summer events, where teachers could get professional development credits for participating. It was very fundamental material about PDCA, problem solving, and meeting facilitation—basically, our Quality Circle program curriculum.

With that in mind, I began to study and prepare to become a trainer. Then, five months after leaving my group leader position, I got a call from TMMK Human Resources asking if I would be interested in working on a part-time basis with a group that was teaching these basic concepts in the Scott County school system. I was pleased to be able to get out there and begin to share what I had learned.

This was another comfort zone challenge, and I will honestly say I struggled in the first few weeks, wondering how making cars could translate to teaching in the classroom, and how we could work with the various administration levels within the school system. Looking back, this was a priceless opportunity that helped me understand that the concepts I had learned in a manufacturing environment could be presented in a very different context.

In the initial stages, the program met with a little resistance, probably because we didn't do an adequate job of explaining the purpose behind the approach. Some educators assumed we were just trying to recruit for Toyota, and that we had minimal understanding about education and what that meant. But some teachers, and also principals and superintendents, were very supportive, and we found that there was a receptive audience that really wanted to learn.

Toyota also genuinely wanted to learn how these ideas could be used to enhance the school curriculum and equip our future workforce with the core competencies that companies like Toyota look for. Consequently, they made a considerable investment in the program. Soon after I began this, TMMK provided some seed money to set up an organization called the Center for Quality People and Organizations (CQPO). The Center, which still operates today, "offers intensive presentations, training programs, planning and design activities, and consultation services that are fully commensurate with the Lean systems and process in use throughout the Toyota Company internationally."

I became a contractor with CQPO, which had established a contract relationship with TMMK and the larger North American organization, which was then known as Toyota Engineering and Manufacturing of America (TEMA). Soon, I was traveling all over the state holding training sessions with various school systems and grade levels. It was another wonderful growth experience. Over the three years I spent doing this, I made all kinds of discoveries about translating the lessons I had learned at TMMK outside of the environment I was used to. I had the wonderful opportunity to teach kids, teachers, and administrators, so there was a lot of thinking about how to present these ideas. When people "got it" and the light bulbs went on, it was really exciting. The kids loved solving problems in teams, and the learning for them, in many cases, was more fun and interactive than what they were used to. And as a bonus, I was getting quite used to getting up to talk in front of people, and becoming more relaxed.

Then came another big moment. As Toyota transitioned many of its Japanese trainers back to their roles in Japan, it needed a way to maintain the integrity and essence of TPS. Since some of CQPO's contractors, including me, had considerable experience as previous TMMK employees, hiring them was a logical choice. CQPO also had a strong leader in executive director Mike Hoseus, a former general manager who later coauthored, with Jeff Liker, *Toyota Culture*.

We began by teaching the Quality Circle Leaders course which I had taken a decade before. At the time, HR was codifying many of the training courses, and they brought us in to help with curriculum development. We taught and helped create course materials for team leader prepromotion training, worksite communication, problem solving, and other subjects. As well, we helped create and taught the four-week course for group leaders, which went into considerable depth in advanced areas such as dealing with conflict, group communication, and the group leader's role in problem solving.

It was very exciting to go back and forth between Toyota and the schools. At TMMK, all the cultural elements were right there in the atmosphere, so many points didn't require a lot of explanation. The schools were different—you really had to start from a different place with different ideas to translate the learning.

Initially, I was using a lot of terminology that I had grown up with at TMMK, including a lot of Japanese words. I learned to avoid those, and the acronyms that went along with them, and to explain in plain English how the concepts worked. I found stories and analogies worked very well, and I still use them today.

I also learned to speak the language of educators. They had intimidated me at first, but once I had learned some of their terms and acronyms and had a better understanding of what they were accountable for, I began to gain confidence in running the sessions. The experience reminded me at times of my initial impressions of the Toyota environment. People had their styles, approaches, and way to do business, just like the various school systems do. So the moment I entered a school environment, I was used to the idea that I had to immerse myself in their world to understand how to best pass knowledge on to them, just as we do today with clients outside of manufacturing.

While all this was progressing, a Lean education community was emerging in the United States. The Lean Enterprise Institute (LEI) was expanding its activities and developing its curriculum. I joined LEI as an independent consultant in 2008, and through that association, began teaching sessions for companies that wanted to learn about Lean. Once again, this was another comfort zone stretch—now I was working in the "big leagues" with people like John Shook. And I really knew I had "made it" in the teaching world when I was asked to teach sessions for Peter Ward in the Master of Business Operational Excellence (MBOE) program at Ohio State University.

A NEW LEARNING COMMUNITY

John Shook, Chairman and CEO, Lean Enterprise Institute

As Toyota's operations gained traction in North America, TPS was becoming so lauded that requests were coming in from all over for the company to share its expertise. However, not surprisingly, as TPS became more and more widely known, associated misunderstandings cropped up as well.

Just in time, for example, was often characterized as a zero inventory strategy that shifted inventory upstream from OEMs to suppliers where it became a burden for them. Quality circles became a fad where casual teams worked on trivial problems unrelated to their work, such as where to place vending machines. In either case, there was no understanding of the true intent of these concepts and practices.

Two organizations emerged from the specific need to satisfy the many requests for support and quell the misunderstandings. The Toyota Supplier Support Center (TSSC) was founded in 1992 under Mr. Cho's direction to provide support to North American companies that wished to adopt TPS. On the outside, author and academic Dr. James Womack formed the Lean Enterprise Institute (LEI) as a not-for-profit publishing, education, and research institute. Both collaborate with Toyota graduates such as Tracey and Ernie who have a passion for sharing the Lean thinking bug.

As I continued on this path, I found myself working with companies that were in various stages of their Lean journey. Some of my first clients came to know me through my work with LEI and wanted me to work with their people to develop a Lean culture. But traveling under the banner of my own company, Teaching Lean, I knew that it was all up to me.

As I mentioned earlier, many people think creating a Lean culture is like waving a magic wand. There are many trainers out there who promise instant results in a variety of subject areas. So I had the task of not only presenting a very different way of thinking, but also getting my learners to understand that their world wasn't going to change overnight.

Since my career at Toyota began when I was 19, this very special environment was the only world I knew. Working to *takt* time, seeing abnormalities, following standards, being aware of each second, and feeling connected to the True North were all things I took for granted.

We knew, for example, that standards were there to help us. We knew that problems were our friends and helped us become better. We knew that there were 27,000 seconds in a shift, and that we had to make these as value-added as possible. It's almost as if there was always a voice in the background, whispering that "there's something abnormal here, and we've got to get on our toes and solve it."

I was initially surprised that these circumstances weren't "normal" in the vast majority of companies. One aha moment came when I was teaching problem solving to a group, and learners were having trouble with the idea of clarifying the problem. I told them to think about the True North, and the purpose of their work. People were confused. "What do you mean by purpose?" they asked. My client, who is now a personal friend, still remembers the shocked look on my face.

As I gained experience, I began to piece together the basic cultural concepts that our trainers at TMMK had passed on to us from very early on, but that are lacking in most organizations.

It was hard at first—these ideas were part of the atmosphere at TMMK, and ingrained in our routines, personal habits, and interactions with coworkers. But by listening to comments and questions from hundreds of participants at my sessions, I began, with Ernie's help, to get a sense of the essential thinking that distinguishes Toyota from the rest of the pack. The more we learned, the better we understood how we could help organizations close the gap between applying Lean tools and adopting the thinking behind the tools.

The Engagement Equation is the result of our learning journey. We'll discuss this in detail in Part 2.

Elements of a
Thinking System

"Go see, ask why, show respect."
—**Fujio Cho**

4

Discipline and Accountability: The Key to Continuous Improvement Thinking

■ ■ ■

As I began to develop in my role of helping other companies improve, I was faced with a major challenge: How could I teach the *thinking* behind the methods that were so successfully implemented at Toyota? I knew that the wisdom that our trainers had so carefully passed on to us was essential to the results that we were all able to create there. Over time, this way of thinking and acting had become more intrinsic to us all, transforming at a very fundamental level how we did our work and how we interacted with others at all levels in the organization.

However, by the time I started Teaching Lean Inc., Toyota's production methods had become very popular as standalone tools, and all too often, there was little or no reference to the culture that supports them at Toyota. I wondered how I could fill this gap.

Ernie and I began to share some ideas about this, and when he retired from Toyota in 2013, he joined me as a full-time partner at Teaching Lean.

Of course, nobody can actually "teach" wisdom—all you can do is guide people as they acquire it, often through practice, direct observation, reflection, and the process of trial and error. With this in mind, Ernie and I began to reflect on the basic principles that could help a learner adopt the thinking that was so critical to our success. The Engagement Equation, which took us 10 years and thousands of teaching hours to develop, is the result of that reflection.

The end result of the equation is something we call DNA—an acronym for discipline and ('n') accountability. DNA is analogous to biological DNA, the genetic code representing the characteristics that define an individual. In using "DNA" to describe the elements of a business culture, we're saying that culture is the sum total of what is going on in the heart and mind of every employee. The equation, therefore, is a tool for instilling the thinking behind the workplace culture, one employee at a time.

Of course, there's a great deal involved with what we are calling DNA. It's about teamwork, respect, safety, standards, and a commitment to always improving your work processes. We're not pretending for a moment that this equation offers any easy answers. In fact, as you will see, DNA calls for all people, from team member to CEO, to pursue goals beyond what they thought they were capable of.

IT'S NOT JUST ABOUT TOOLS

Bret Kindler, Former Corporate
Lean Specialist, The Timken Company

The big difference in Tracey's and Ernie's workshops on problem solving is their emphasis on culture.

The idea is that you can't do problem solving without doing coaching. You can't just drop the tool on somebody and say, "Go do it." It doesn't work like that. It has to be part of your life, and part of what you do. So it's really a people development tool more than anything else. This is the part that really gets people saying, "Wow, this is a lot different than what I ever thought it was," and it's the reason we've been able to take this much further than we expected.

ALWAYS IMPROVING IS THE NEW NORMAL

In competitive markets, companies must continuously evolve. If a company like Apple wants to just maintain its market share, it has to innovate all the time, and if it wants to actually gain market share, it has to move even faster.

When Apple came out with the first iPhone, there weren't a lot of similar products out there, but now look at it. There are all kinds of competing products that are giving Apple a run for its money. And so, as the market evolves, people at Apple are constantly asking, "How can we improve so that we'll be better than our competitors?"

During our time at TMMK, Toyota was gaining market share very quickly, especially in North America, and we were constantly looking for ways to improve our products. Imagine what it would have been like if we had stayed the same, celebrating all of our successes on the KPI boards. If Toyota still produced the 1988 version of the Camry today, how would that model fare in today's market, with all the expectations about modern bells and whistles? Probably about as well, maybe, as a 1988 cell phone.

The market always wants something new. It wants heated seats, it wants voice command technology, parking assist, backup cameras, and blind spot monitors. And guess what? It's not too keen on having to pay more. So Camrys and Corollas haven't gone up that much in price over the years, but Toyota has added a lot of value in add-on features that it isn't charging for.

Of course, Toyota made some Apple-like innovative leaps as well. When the Prius was introduced in 1999, it was, like the iPhone, a first. Today, hybrid electric vehicles (HEVs) are old news, but nobody has come close to catching up with Toyota. This is because people at Toyota are continually thinking, "How can we make these even better, and offer more value for less money?" These questions were part of DNA, and were on everybody's mind as we constantly strove to improve our work processes.

CREATING BETTER VALUE

When you look at this at the highest level, there are only two things we can do to improve the value we create for our customers:

1. Do the same amount of work with fewer man hours.
2. Do more value added with the same man hours.

There are probably some nuances in the middle, but basically, that's it.

Neither of these is finite—they go on forever as we continuously meet targets and raise the bar. When we first started at TMMK, it took several days to convert the line for a model change. We had to stop the line, move flow racks in and out, and then run the new model.

What's it like today? Well on average, there are 5 to 10 minutes—that's right, minutes—between model changes, depending upon factors such as line configuration, model mix, or differences between the plants. And with three or four models running simultaneously at TMMK, there is always a minor or major model change going on with one of them, requiring a constant level of PDCA thinking.

Think about that—from days down to minutes! Whether you look at the additional cars that can be made, the additional profit, or the productivity of each worker, that's a lot of resources. But the bottom line is when we reduce the time spent getting ready to make cars as opposed to actually making cars, we free up those additional resources to either make each of those cars more valuable or reduce their cost, benefiting the company and the customer.

But what do you think the trainers said when they got to this point? Do you think they wiped their brows and thought that was enough? Not a chance. Toyota may be one of the world's most successful manufacturers, but we can guarantee you that one of the first things the trainer said when they reached that 60-second *takt* time was, "Are we able to achieve a lower *takt* time if the customer needs us to produce more?"

Every day, there's that sense of urgency, no matter what was accomplished the day before. Every single day, that idea of continuous improvement was essential to our business. We define this as E^3—Everybody Everyday Engaged—and we'll discuss this in detail in Part 3.

Of course, all this sounds pretty exhausting, and when we talk about this in our seminars, we get a lot of hands going up. In a recent workshop, a participant asked this question: "So how does Toyota combat this potential fatigue that comes out of that cycle of always raising the bar, and never actually reaching a destination until we already are off to the next one? Doesn't this create frustration?"

I explained that although the need to constantly improve may initially seem daunting for the leaders and the people involved, it actually reduces frustration and anxiety once that thinking becomes a conditioned norm. The idea here is that if I can continue to fix problems, determine measures, improve processes, and set standards, then the company has a much greater opportunity for long-term sustainability and growth, strengthening its ability to provide long-term employment. To summarize:

Problems Solved = Job Security

So we jokingly say to companies, "If it weren't for problems, how many people would your company actually need?" It really makes you think for a second, and it's a powerful incentive for adopting a problem-solving frame of mind.

In fact, this is exactly the kind of motivator that makes people feel empowered as they come to work each day. It's when people don't understand the "purpose" behind their work that you have to worry about fatigue, demotivation, and cultural difficulties. Psychologists have been telling us this for a long time.

A PROGRAM FOR DEVELOPING LEADERS

Peter Ward, Director, Center for Operational Excellence and Professor of Management Sciences, Ohio State University

We have been on our own journey in terms of teaching about operational excellence for more than 20 years, and for the past nine we've offered a master's degree in operational excellence. Our program includes a mix of students from all over the country, and many different industries and settings, including service and healthcare as well as manufacturing.

At our very first meeting, each student brings a significant problem that they're going to work on for the entire year. Tracey and Ernie kick off the program by talking about problems, and about how to approach that specific problem in terms of thinking about it, breaking it down, and making sense of it. This really gets us off on a footing that we try to live up to each and every time we get together.

THE VALUE OF EVERY SECOND

You can see from what you've read so far that profound respect for standards was a given in our environment. Time was very much the essence here, and this was reflected in TMMK's attendance policy that was in force when we first started.

I learned about this the hard way back in the days when I was a new team member. One day, I arrived at my process 30 seconds late. I knew from my new hire orientation about our start and stop times for first shift, and how important it was to be on time, but I had just assumed I would get a pass if it was just a few seconds late.

I was a little surprised, then, when I was asked to meet with my group leader later that day to discuss how I was going to cover my "lost time." In our discussion, I was reminded that in order to ensure that quality and productivity expectations were met, a team leader had to cover over half my process. Even though my absence was very brief, it was still an absence that triggered a necessary action by my team leader.

I quickly internalized this, as did my fellow team members, and developed the habit of being at my work process on time, fully dressed in my PPE (personal protective equipment). Furthermore, I set my mind to achieving perfect attendance, as there were rewards for that.

Now, when I share this story with people who are unfamiliar with Toyota's culture, many folks jump to the conclusion that TMMK (Toyota) policies are insensitive to people and overly rigid with standards. Many are used to thinking, "Who cares if I'm 30 seconds late? Even if I'm 30 minutes late, it shouldn't make that much difference. I will just make up my time later in the day or come in early the next morning."

The point is, every team member at TMMK plays an essential role in supporting the overall output, and every second counts. Respect for each of those seconds isn't something you can turn on and off when it is convenient—you really have to live up to the expectations they were created from. And as we will see, this is a big part of what we call DNA.

The attendance policy, therefore, was connected with a deeper purpose. The unsaid message here was, "Tracey-san, you are a contributor to our Plastics team, which ensures our Assembly shop internal customer has all their expectations met. We need your contribution so we can set the stage for the external customer to have a smile."

Getting that smile from the external customer depended on individuals in all functional areas within TMMK (Toyota) understanding their role in the "order to customer" value stream. When you truly embrace the meaning and cost translation of a second of time, it's the pathway to purpose.

As Eiji Toyoda says in the Toyota Way, "People are the most important asset to a company, they are also the determinant of the rise and fall of an organization." The attendance policy, seen in this light, respects the true value of each and every individual to the organization. And when you consider how deeply TMMK invested in us, there can be no question about its commitment to this way of thinking.

Let's get back to that 30 seconds for a moment. Remember our journey to get model changes down from several days to several minutes?

Here's another example. When we started at TMMK, the expectation was that we'd be able to send a new car off the line every 60 seconds. We found this unbelievable—even 65 seconds seemed nearly impossible in those early days—but little did we know that several years down the road, we would see the *takt* standard drop as low as 53 seconds.

This was achieved, literally, one second at a time, and every employee contributed ideas to move us forward. Our trainers taught us that the key to improvement wasn't trying to hit a home run every time—it was about getting lots of base hits, and finding ways to minimize errors and avoid repeating mistakes.

As well, it was about looking for ways to improve every single day. That's how Toyota achieves its phenomenal results.

One of my first trainers illustrated this point by challenging us to observe and discover one second of waste at our processes. This seemed at first to be a joke to me, but I quickly realized no one was laughing. We Instrument Panel (I/P) team members glanced at each other with a puzzled look, because many of us were thinking, "Is a second really so important that we need to spend our time searching for one?" We felt we could use our time more wisely—what an assumption that was!

Our trainer, sensing our skepticism, said, "Let me explain the importance of one second to this company (TMMK)." So we all gathered around a flipchart out by the process, and he began to jot down a few numbers. He explained that if every team member in the entire plant, not just our I/P team, saved a second of time, the accumulated savings would allow us to produce eight more Camrys in a single shift.

I wondered, "How could this be possible?" But when you accounted for all the variables—number of employees, number of processes, seconds in each cycle, etc.—and did the math, eight Camrys per shift was the correct number.

I don't know the exact impact on profitability, but one can assume that eight cars per shift with no additional investment is going to make a significant difference to the company. And it provides a definitive "yes" to the question, "Could what I do each day be that important to the overall company output?" This message was very empowering, and it helped us internalize just how important our jobs were.

What's exciting here is that TMMK, by placing continuous improvement in the hands of the workforce, was assigning enormous responsibility to each and every worker—essentially, they were entrusting us with the value of those precious seconds, which cumulatively added up to significant benefits for both the company and our customers.

This reinforced our understanding of DNA, and our commitment to "go thinking," a phrase that we used at the time and is now printed on the back of our business cards. And yes, it showed that being 30 seconds late really does make a difference.

THE MEANING OF STANDARDS

Taiichi Ohno taught us that there can be no improvement without standards. I like to think of the standard as *the best known documented method at a given moment that we all agree to be accountable to until we improve it together.* Once an improvement has been made, it's up to every worker to maintain that standard. Showing up on time for work, therefore, was only one of many standards that we were expected to follow at Toyota.

Looking at the big picture, the standard of 60 seconds was really the sum and total of literally thousands of local standards. We had standards for how long each part of our process took, down to the second. We had standards for safety, quality, ergonomics, and mental burden. We had standards for how we held our tools, how we as leaders reviewed each and every one of our processes, and how we interacted with each of our team members. In fact, the number of standards we had to internalize is a great illustration of the extraordinary commitment behind DNA.

Now, it's important to point out here that standards aren't just about making cars faster. TMMK was equally concerned with avoiding stress and monotony for workers. To that end, Ohno also said, "Why not make the work easier and more interesting so that people do not have to sweat?" The Toyota style is not to improve results by working harder—it is, as Deming said, about working smarter. It is a way of thinking that says there is no limit to people's creativity when it comes to improving their processes. We might say that people don't come to Toyota every day to work, they come there to think. In a similar vein, we like to think of Toyota as a company that develops people first, and just happens to make cars!

"EIGHT YOU'RE FINE, NINE YOU'RE MINE"

From a psychological standpoint, our relationship with standards can be fairly complex. Let's look at an example that we're all familiar with—speed limits.

Every road you drive on is going to have a speed limit. Even on a back road with no signs, you have to follow the stated limit. Now, it's not unusual for people to break the law at some time or other. Sometimes it's knowingly, sometimes it's unknowingly. Maybe we're just in a hurry, we're not paying attention, or it's "wait a minute, the zone changed, it went down." But there's no confusion about what the law says, and in our system, ignorance of the law is no excuse.

Of course, speed limits have a purpose—to ensure that our roads are safe. The problem is, we may feel that the standard is too restricting for our purposes. So we figure out what the limits are, and what we can get away with. If we go a few miles per hour too fast, law enforcement will probably leave us alone. In Kentucky, we often hear the expression, "Eight you're fine, nine you're mine."

People tend to set their own standards based on that expectation—maybe they set the cruise control at 8 mph over the limit. Or maybe they take a bit of a risk now and then—there certainly aren't enough cops on the road to catch everybody who is speeding. Whether or not the standard is followed, therefore, is subject to a degree of personal choice at this point.

Now let's look at this through a different lens. What if your state, or your province, passed a zero-tolerance law—say, you'd lose your driver's license if an officer caught you going one mile per hour over the limit? Behaviors would change in a hurry.

People would be pretty careful, and nobody would pass you going 15 miles per hour faster. You just wouldn't take that risk, even if there wasn't a cop in sight.

We can often get a similar respect for a law or standard when we reflect on its purpose. For instance, we all know the feeling of frustration we get when we drive into a construction zone and the speed limit drops from, say, 60 mph to 45 mph. But if we think for a moment about the construction workers that are working very close to the roadway, and their families who are waiting for them to return home safely, that 45 mph takes on a very different meaning.

All of this illustrates the mindset behind our relationship with standards. It's a deeply ingrained idea at Toyota that standards are something all workers are committed to, whether it's showing up for work exactly on time, or any of the other standards that we have to maintain every day. This is not a matter of personal choice.

Furthermore, we were deeply connected with the "why" behind the standards, and how fulfillment of that purpose depends on all of us. A constant reminder for us was the fact that in the Toyota Production System, a deviation from standard may well cause a line to be shut down. So that constant awareness of standards on the part of every employee literally keeps the plant running.

Of course, there's no way a trainer or a manager could possibly enforce all the standards we had to follow, and this leads us to another important point: *DNA is how people behave when nobody's looking.*

DNA, therefore, has to be learned, absorbed, lived, and breathed. The constant awareness that comes with that is something we internalize to the point where we don't even think about it. Ernie and I never lost that, and even today, we take it home with us. If you come to our house in Ormond Beach, Florida, you'll see standardization everywhere. It's how we might prepare meals, use a *kanban* system for groceries, and organize our work and living areas. Even our cat knows what our standards are all about, and he has his own as well!

People often ask us, "How could you survive in such a rigid environment?" We answer that acquiring DNA is a little like getting in shape at the gym. It's tough at first, but when you work at it for a while, it becomes part of your daily routine, and soon, you start to enjoy the benefits. Ultimately, DNA makes it possible for everybody to work as a team toward a common True North—a "fitness goal" that is truly worth achieving.

STANDARDS FOR MAKING CHANGES

As we've shown, the environment at TMMK was constantly changing, and we were all trained to be active participants in that change, whether it was making a small adjustment to a work process or participating in a major model change.

As problem solvers and change agents, it was critical that we followed a standard procedure when we made changes so that all those affected would be on the same page. Getting everybody to understand and internalize a common approach to problem solving was therefore central to development of people at TMMK. This involved, essentially, coaching and teaching by example through actions that aligned with the PDCA mindset and supported the True North of the company.

Usually, the problems encountered in the workplace were small and could be addressed on the spot through a simplified form of PDCA thinking. Sometimes, however, a change would affect multiple stakeholders, which meant that a number of people had to understand the proposed change and provide input and support. To accomplish this, we had a standard process for documenting the change process so that everybody affected could be on the same page.

The method we used is called A3, named for the double-sized, 11×17 sheet that the report is usually presented on. The A3

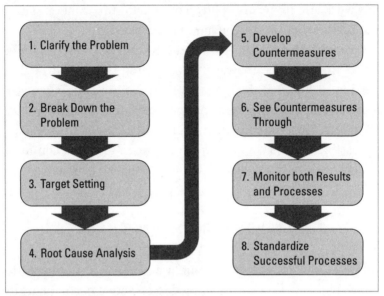

FIGURE 4.1 A3 problem-solving process

method follows the eight-step problem-solving process we used internally, which was closely modeled on PDCA (Figure 4.1). The eight steps expand on the PDCA principle, creating a powerful sequence of actions that ensure that the scientific discipline behind PDCA is properly maintained throughout. The eight steps prescribe certain actions, but more important, they reflect a way of thinking that is central to the realization of Toyota's values.

This eight-step process itself, which became known as Toyota Business Practices (TBP) in the early 2000s, underwent considerable improvements over three decades under the supervision of our leader, Fujio Cho. Although we didn't use TBP in its codified form in my area at the time I was a leader, I can honestly say that I grew along with the evolution of these ideas and was blessed to learn the wisdom behind TBP from the originators in my role as a Toyota Institute Certified Trainer.

Today, the eight steps are taught as follows, showing the corresponding PDCA steps.

1. Clarify the problem (P)
2. Break down the problem (P)
3. Target setting (P)
4. Root cause analysis (P)
5. Develop countermeasures (P)
6. See countermeasures through (D)
7. Monitor both results and processes (C)
8. Standardize successful processes (A)

As we follow the eight steps through the PDCA cycle, we use A3 to create a document that others can see and understand easily. This form of "standardized storytelling" is key within any culture practicing PDCA thinking and can be a powerful tool to engage and empower leaders as well as the front lines. The A3 cuts across all functional silos and can become the common language for successful Lean transformation. I like to call this "Lean communication," or a "5S of information," enabling you to share your thinking with others. People don't need to know everything you did to get there, just the key points that show the logic of the steps and the meaning behind them.

The steps show just how much time we spent planning. My trainer once said that if there was a project that took 12 months, we would spend 9 months planning and 3 months implementing. He jokingly said other companies usually did the opposite—planned for 3 months and had a very frustrating 9-month implementation with a lot of rework. The trainers encouraged us to always invest in planning and following the process. This can be often be the determining factor in whether or not a project adds value to the organization.

The common A3 format was applied in many situations. We had A3s for problem solving, improvement, and strategy, and the same method could be applied at all levels of the organization. However, regardless of the scope of the project, we never lost sight of our main priority, which was developing people.

The main goal for A3s, therefore, was to "share wisdom" (the thinking of others) in order to develop people with a common lens, and learning was always at the forefront of our work with A3s. Often, within the A3 process we used a process called "catch-ball," where the A3 traveled back and forth between leaders and workers, each offering insights based on their perspectives. When the project was complete, the A3 served as a written record of lessons learned and improvements made. We then shared it with other affected areas that the idea could assist in improving a process. Internally, this was called *yokoten*, and it was an expectation that was embedded in step 8 of the TBP process.

Perhaps the most important aspect of this is that it's the thinking behind the paper, not the A3 paper itself, that is most important. The written A3 can never be the result of just filling out a form—by filling the squares, we are effectively verifying the thinking, and that we have asked the appropriate questions of ourselves and our coworkers in the process, and shown due respect to all of the people involved, regardless of their role or function in the organization.

However, as mentioned, not all projects required a written A3. As we discussed earlier, continuous improvement is a game of mostly base hits, and the occasional home run. We would determine whether to write an A3 based on factors such as the severity of the problem, the number of stakeholders involved, resource requirements, and, of course, the potential learning opportunity.

After solving problems for a number of years, I got to the point where I knew intrinsically what I had to do and what questions I had to ask in about 70 percent of the cases. Therefore, I didn't use the written format a lot of the time. However, it was a given that I always followed the A3 thinking to the letter. When my leaders did request an A3 of me it was usually to share my wisdom with others.

This intuitive understanding that we all developed about problem solving was essential. However, when companies emulate Toyota, they tend to implement the steps, but not the thinking that made them work. As a result, the A3 in many organizations is little more than a form that people fill out, and the steps are "check box" items rather than reflections of any kind of real thinking. Some organizations even have quotas for the "paper A3," while giving only lip service to the value-added thinking behind the paper.

THE ENGAGEMENT EQUATION

Our life's work today is to fill this critical gap by bringing Toyota's unique *thinking* to life in the training room, conference session, or *gemba*. We developed the Engagement Equation, $GTS^6 + E^3 = DNA$, to help learners grasp and internalize the cultural concepts that were so essential to our daily work in an environment where it was considered everybody's job to continually look for improvement, solve problems, and above all, develop our most important asset—people.

When people see that we're introducing an equation, they might conclude that this is a "wave the wand" approach. In fact, this couldn't be further from the truth! As you saw in Part 1, we all succeeded together at TMMK only with incredibly hard work that challenged us to do things we never would have believed we could do. So the equation is, in many ways, a reminder of the many challenges that have to be confronted daily with this approach.

The basic thinking here applies at all levels of the organization, whether the employee is the CEO making an executive decision or an hourly worker making an improvement to a shop-floor process. This versatility reflects the true meaning of DNA and the spirit behind the lessons we were taught at Toyota.

It explains how a company from Japan was able to mold 8,000 workers from rural Kentucky into a team of 8,000 problem solvers and together win the J.D. Power Gold Plant Award only a year and a half after the start of production.

It took us about 10 years of trial and error to develop the equation. We have refined it through feedback from hundreds of participants in our sessions who had exhorted us to provide them with something that would help them internalize all that they had learned. The equation is not perfect, but it has proven to be an accurate and effective tool in helping individuals and organizations assimilate the cultural elements that we acquired during our years at TMMK.

Let's look at the equation:

$$GTS^6 + E^3 = DNA$$

The equation represents what we have to do to instill DNA throughout the organization.

GTS represents each of the elements of problem solving. GTS^6 represents six different GTS acronyms that all work together. They are:

- **Go to See.** Get away from your desk. Instead of relying on conference room meetings, find out what is really happening at the *gemba*. Develop a keen eye for waste and problems that aren't immediately obvious. Listen to what your people are telling you. Always question your assumptions. Always keep purpose in mind when you visit the *gemba*.
- **Grasp the Situation.** Gather the facts about what is actually happening versus what should be happening, and determine in a scientific way exactly how that gap can be measured. Ask questions that uncover facts, not opinions. Break down problems into manageable components.
- **Get to Solution.** Determine root causes and formulate an action plan that removes the problem. Make sure the

plan addresses all the facts and doesn't jump to conclusions. Develop consensus among all stakeholders, and maintain consensus and thorough communication as you implement the plan.

- **Get to Standardization.** Develop the work standard so that the successful practice can be universally adopted across the organization. Ensure that the standard is properly communicated, understood, and followed with accountability.

- **Get to Sustainability.** Make sure that the solution remains stable. Review results carefully to ensure that they are not reverting to the old norm. Use leading indicators to identify any factors that might destabilize the process or make it obsolete.

- **Get to Stretch.** Raise the bar, and start over again. Remember that it is essential to always be improving.

We will look at all six GTSs in detail in the following chapters, within the context of the problem-solving process. It's important to distinguish method from thinking here. The eight-step process, or PDCA, is the method of solving a particular problem, and the progression through these steps is the journey that every problem solver must take.

GTS^6, on the other hand, represents the mindsets that we carry with us as we go through all the steps. These occur and reoccur at various stages, and as the problem-solving process intensifies and involves more people, more of these GTS mindsets come into play. This will all become clear in the following chapters.

E^3, the other term in the equation, stands for Everybody Everyday Engaged. It signifies that leaders must engage every employee in GTS^6 so that this thinking becomes a way of life across the entire organization. It represents the leadership standardized work for engaging people so that all understand and apply this thinking.

We will discuss E^3 in detail in Part 3 when we talk about the role of leaders in the organization.

So in a nutshell, this is the equation for the kind of thinking that everybody has to be engaged in. $GTS^6 + E^3$ is the process, and DNA is the outcome.

THE FORMULA THAT DRIVES US

Tanya Doyle, Lean Culture Coach

I have that formula posted on my wall by my stand-up desk, and it drives me every day. It drives me to go out there, go to see, grasp the situation, get to solution, all those things. Multiple times a day, I point to it on the wall and say to people, "Guys, this is the DNA for success." It's like, "Hey, pay attention. It's this simple, it's really this simple." It's a brilliant formula in my opinion. It just works.

We'll close here with a couple of caveats. First of all, is critical to see the totality of this approach. Like any equation, its elements cannot be bypassed for the sake of time or results. As well, you will get out of the process as much as you are willing to invest.

And once again, we make no claim that this is going to be easy. Learning the concepts represented in the equation requires initiative on the part of all participants, and we can guarantee that setbacks will be part of the learning process. Some of the steps are counterintuitive at first, and don't fully make sense without a lot of practice. We warn you, it's going to be like those first few times you go to the gym. But like fitness, the effort is well worth it, and the effort invested will pay off in the long run.

Let's get to work.

5

Go to See

■ ■ ■

Once upon a time, there was an automotive manufacturer called Reliable Motor Manufacturing. The company had an excellent reputation for quality. It followed the Toyota Production System very closely and had been taught by some of the best Lean consultants in the land. Clayton, its VP of Manufacturing, was a strong Lean supporter and a true servant leader. Reliable was considered a Lean success story, and people came from miles around to visit its plant.

After some successful years, Clayton began to get the feeling that not all was right at Reliable. Somehow, the energy behind continuous improvement and problem solving was not what it had been a few years ago. People had all the tools and all the training, but there was something missing in the atmosphere. Clayton consulted with his Lean leaders, and they agreed that there was something lacking in the culture, but they couldn't quite put their finger on it. Clayton knew that he would have to get personally involved if this problem was to be solved.

Now, living in the same town was a wise sensei who was known to a few insiders in the Lean community. His name was Kadan Brody; however, those who had worked with him referred to him as Brody-san. Little was known about him other than that he had a very deep knowledge of the Toyota Production System, which he preferred to call the Thinking Production System, and an understanding of Toyota's culture that amazed even people who had worked at Toyota for many years.

Encouraged by his team, Clayton went to see this wise man and told him about his company in great detail. Mr. Brody listened patiently to everything Clayton had to say. He was different from the management consultants that Clayton had met with in that he didn't seem to be jumping forward with answers. When Clayton had finished, he asked Mr. Brody, "We use all of Toyota's methods, and I have done everything my Lean experts have asked me to do to support continuous improvement, but we seem to be losing the momentum that we worked so hard to create. I have heard that you understand the thinking behind Toyota's cultural DNA. Can I hire you to come in and fix our culture?"

Mr. Brody was silent for a long time. "I can't fix your culture," he said. "I wish I was that good. All I can do is work with you to help you evolve your culture. This will take much hard work from you and all your people."

Clayton was impatient, but he was also wise enough to not expect instant answers. "My team and I are ready for anything it takes," said Clayton. "We are completely committed."

"Very well," said Mr. Brody, "I will try to help you. But there will be two conditions. First, you share information openly with me and allow me to engage freely with your people."

"Agreed," said Clayton without hesitation.

"The second is that you must accept a different way of thinking that will change how you interact with your people."

Clayton knew that the best Lean *sensei* require this, and he was ready. "Yes," he said, "I have already discussed this with my team. We are all here to learn and absorb your wisdom."

"Very well," said Mr. Brody, "I will be in your office before your first shift on Monday morning. And by the way, since we will be working together closely, please call me Brody-san."

Now, even with his grueling schedule as a VP of manufacturing, Clayton wasn't used to getting up at 4:30 a.m. But he was very excited to have Brody-san coming into his company, so he agreed to meet Brody-san at 6:00 a.m. on Monday morning.

"I will have everything ready for you," he said. "I'll have HR run off all the reports from our employee surveys. I will also instruct IT to give you access to all of our manufacturing data and our financials."

"I won't need any of that right now," said Brody-san. "Before we can do anything, we must get some facts about your culture. And to do that, we must Go to See together."

AN EARLY LESSON

In my early days as a team leader, I noticed that my trainers, during a short visit, were able to see waste in my processes that I hadn't been able to see for many weeks. I felt in the beginning that they were somehow born with an innate ability to see waste or abnormality. As I learned later, they had to work hard to acquire this skill just as we did, so they understood what we were going through.

In fact, when our trainer came to our area, his top priority was to pass on this wonderful skill of looking deeply at what was right in front of us. As Mr. Cho used to say, "It is your responsibility as a leader to share wisdom with the next generation." I truly feel that my trainers lived the spirit of these words, and that it is my duty to do the same.

We weren't given a documented set of instructions for Go to See at TMMK, and we didn't have fancy terms to describe it either—we were leading and learning as we matured as individuals and as a company. It was crystal clear, however, that Go to See helped us differentiate facts from assumptions, paving the way to properly frame our problems, as we will learn about in the next chapter.

Our early lessons in Go to See began in the start-up phase, before we even began to roll salable cars off the line. As mentioned earlier, I was in the Plastics department making instrument panels, and Ernie, who received the same lesson in a different context, was making axles for chassis assembly in the Powertrain department.

With instrument panels, we had to cut openings for the air vents, the radio, and various items on the steering column, and the specifications were very strict. We also had to remove burrs and other residue from the cutting process—something that's called deflashing.

Sometimes we wondered why the specifications had to be so strict, and we started asking questions. At that point, the trainer saw that it was time for a lesson in "Go to See."

They took us, two at a time, to follow a "day in the life" of an instrument panel after we had completed our work. The panels were sequenced and loaded into movable containers 20 at a time, that is, a *kanban* of 20, and sent to our internal customer in assembly.

What we observed on the visit could never have been conveyed in words. Essentially, we saw with our own eyes how our failure to meet the designed specifications would affect the assembly process. For example, if a piece of flash was too long, it could flap underneath the vent and make a fluttering sound when the air conditioner was on. And that's not something our customer, internal or external, would be happy about!

Of course, these assembly people had to worry about their customers, so they too had to meet very tight specifications. If something didn't match perfectly, this might add 5, 10, or 15 seconds to their process. It could even create a situation for an *andon* pull that could lead to a line stoppage.

The real lesson is that once we got back to our own process, things looked different. The specification for cutting that hole wasn't just a spec—it was our guide for ensuring that our customer down the line was not going to have a problem. Knowing the purpose removed any perception that we were following specification just because the leader said so. I don't think I viewed my processes in quite the same way after that experience.

Ernie was taken through a similar exercise in the Powertrain department. He learned that the visual markings on the upper support of the axle were crucial for the assembly worker to install the axle without the wasteful action of fixing misalignments.

Having a keen awareness of the relationship between our work and customer needs was really the first step in Go to See. In this case, the work that our internal customers were doing was the "why" behind the specifications. But sometimes, the "why" could only be revealed one way—by going to see. And after going to see, we could now visualize our own processes in a deeper way while helping to build mutual trust and respect with our coworkers in other departments.

THE LONG TRADITION OF GOING TO SEE

John Shook, Chairman and CEO, Lean Enterprise Institute

There's a longstanding tradition in Japan to not trust words. This stems from the very Zen idea that words don't capture experience. When Toyota formally codified the Toyota Production System in 1973, it was controversial to write it down. Taiichi Ohno himself expressed strong concern by saying that if you name it, you kill it.

However, we all read books, so that's a compromise we accept. And when you start to engage a larger number of people, suppliers, and suppliers' suppliers, the need to communicate overrides the trepidation about assigning labels. This resulted in the codification of TPS, and the publication of *Toyota Way 2001*. But the skepticism has remained, and *sensei* of TPS are very hesitant to make blanket statements or to have the words taken out of context.

MAKING IT EASIER TO SEE

One of the secrets of Go to See is not hiding anything, and everybody takes part in making processes visible. That might sound pretty basic, but when you visit a lot of workplaces, you will see clutter, poor sight lines, inefficient layouts of equipment, stacks of inventory, and poorly designed or poorly maintained display boards. You'll see a lot of waste there, but you can be sure that there's a whole lot more under the surface.

At TMMK, there were very strict standards about maintaining workspaces so that all aspects of the process were clearly visible. As the saying goes, you can't manage what you can't measure, and it is equally true that you can't manage what you can't see. So in our workspace, sight lines were clear, tools were always in their proper place, equipment was clearly marked, and all safety requirements were highly visible.

These practices included our offices as well. In nonmanufacturing departments, we used these principles to control office supplies. Personal desks were expected to meet a certain standard, and there were maximums and minimums on office supplies—pens, paper clips, staples, etc.—to help minimize waste and control costs.

We were also taught from very early on to keep visual charts that helped us and any observer look deeper into the processes. One of these is called a Yamazumi chart. Basically, it's a stacked bar chart (or cycle bar chart) that illustrates various aspects of a process such as:

- Wait time
- Walk time
- Process time
- Machine time
- Setup time
- Rework/repair
- Delay work
- Wait *kanban* time

These displays are often generated on computers, but at TMMK, we used stacked magnets on a white display board to track the time required for various work elements. A horizontal line going across the center of the display represents the standard *takt* expectation so we are clearly able to see the gaps at a glance. This allows the trainer to rebalance or *kaizen* in order to meet the internal and external customer expectation. It's a great visual tool for seeing abnormality very quickly, and helps team members in the process understand at a glance where they are in regard to the standard.

When our trainers looked at these visual charts, they were also thinking beyond the standards to potential areas for improvement. Some of the considerations were:

- Process capacity
- Machine capacity
- Manpower capacity/level loading
- *Takt* time (Are we meeting customer demand consistently?)
- Mix capabilities/level loading

There are many more aspects of this, but the main point is that the entire work environment was designed to prevent waste and abnormalities from being hidden, and also to make it easier for our trainers to look deeper into the processes, and to teach us to do the same.

LOW-TECH VISUAL MANAGEMENT

Jon Miller, Co-Founder, Gemba Academy

Toyota has a bias for low-tech visual management tools that dates back to the development of the Toyota Production System, before PCs were widely used. The bias has survived for several reasons. First of all, Toyota prefers that engineers and supervisors remain in their *gemba* and do not retreat to their offices to update their visuals on a computer. Second, pen-and-paper visuals allow the people who do the work to easily design, modify, and update them. Finally, Toyota prefers not to invest in a fancy digital display board when a simple system of handwritten numbers with red and green status lamps will do just fine. While it is not bad to progress to a technological solution, it is not acceptable to start there and then be unable to change course because of the investment already made.

THE GUIDING LIGHT

Another critical piece here is the deep sense of purpose that was part of the culture at TMMK. In other words, our trainers knew why we were doing the work we were doing. So when we would Go to See, we didn't do it in a vacuum—we were always thinking about the purpose behind the work, and how what we did each day contributed to the key performance indicators of the company.

Seeing this connection with the company's goals is something we called line of sight. While there may be mitigating conditions such as economic fluctuations, material disruptions, etc., the True North, that is, the vision, purpose, and mission, always remains the same.

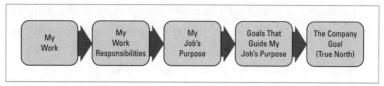

FIGURE 5.1 Line of sight

We use the diagram shown in Figure 5.1 to depict line of sight in our sessions. Awareness of this was instilled from day one at TMMK. Everything we did had a purpose, and as we gained experience, that line of sight got clearer and clearer. But the point is, whether you are looking at a worker installing a mirror or developing a human resources policy, there is always a connection between that and the True North, and Go to See must always reflect this connection.

So regardless of what activity we were engaged in, we were conditioned to ask, how are you measuring, and how will you know when you get there? Both should align upward.

LOOKING DEEPER

When I became a team leader, I thought I had developed a good eye at Going to See, and by conventional standards, I certainly had. At TMMK, however, there was always a trainer looking for the opportunity to teach you a deeper lesson, even with your years of experience.

Let's look at a more advanced exercise that I experienced as a leader. We were making headliners, that is, the roof panel in the interior of the car. Our trainers had been asking us to shave about 4 or 5 seconds off one of the processes where the headliner is pressed. This is the process where we cut out openings for the reading lamp above the back, the lamps above the seats, etc. This took, as I recall, about 58 seconds.

Our trainer asked us where we could see some waste. He had a couple of ideas, we felt, but of course, he wanted us to go through the learning of seeing it ourselves.

We found this really challenging. The process looked pretty solid in terms of value added. There was not a lot of walk time—everything seemed to be within a couple of steps, or a couple of hand-width links. We were saying, "Wow—I don't know where we're going to find these 4 or 5 seconds."

Our trainer asked, "What are all the contributing factors? Machine? Part? Person?" This was tough—we didn't see anything, and we kept looking back at him as if we were playing "hot and cold." He kept asking us questions, and then he started asking about the equipment.

Now, equipment wasn't something I was used to thinking about. Whether we call it accepted norms or tribal knowledge, I wasn't asking the right questions. I figured the machine is what it is because that's how it's designed.

Our trainer began to ask deeper questions about the machine and the nuances around it. We could see that sometimes the worker had to wait a second for the gate to open, but this was outside of our skill set. But he persisted. "Look at the mold travel as the press is opening up," he said. "What do you think?"

We hadn't considered this, because we thought it had to be that way. We had assumed that when it came to altering things, anything to do with maintenance, tools and dies, or design of equipment was off-limits.

The lesson, of course, is that in order to grasp all the contributing factors involved, you have to ask. This allows you to know which stakeholders you may need for potential changes.

So we continued to study further and, guided by our trainer, looked at the amount of time that it took the mold to travel to its fixed stop position. Of course, there had to be a safety allowance to avoid potential head injury to the workers doing their job. But with that taken into account, the headliner mold was opening way too far.

Once we had determined the necessary opening width, we realized that maintenance could reprogram the equipment to reduce the travel distance. That extra distance was costing 4 seconds of machine time, which in turn could also cause a person to wait. By looking deeply at the situation, we were able to eliminate that 4 seconds of wait time and still meet spec.

Of course, this is not always possible. A machine may well be set up in a particular way to meet a specification for safety, quality, or productivity, but you can always ask. In this case, the machine was likely set up according to the best information that people had at the time, but that didn't mean it had to stay that way.

This can be a challenge in nonmanufacturing environments as well, where we often see the same assumptions about our IT systems. We might assume, for example, that it's necessary to have three screens of input because "that's how the system works," but if we look deeper, we may learn that those three can be reduced to one without compromising the process.

THE BIGGEST BARRIER TO SEEING—
OUR OWN ASSUMPTIONS

Are you aware of whether each decision you make at the workplace is based on a fact, or on an assumption? I believe you would be amazed at how many fall into the latter category.

The problem is, when we mistake assumptions for facts, we often make very foolish decisions. Taiichi Ohno summarized this very well when he said, *"People's ideas are unreliable things, and I'd be impressed if we're right even half the time."*

Of course, it's easy to take a statement like that and put it on a poster or a wall plaque. But the practice of questioning our assumptions means we have to constantly validate our thinking. Something may seem as clear as day, but we could, on reflection, be looking through the distorted lens of "conventional wisdom."

Our trainers were aware of how difficult this was, even for me after I had become a team leader. So they were patient, but also very persistent about conditioning my thinking to a deeper level of awareness.

This way of managing is not common in most workplaces—in fact, it is quite the opposite. In many companies, people are so used to reacting to results that assumptions are treated like new facts. Many actually believe that stopping to confirm a thought makes people less productive, and that saying, "I don't know" is admitting to weakness. In our view, however, being able to say, "If I don't know, let's go see and learn about it together" shows the true strength and courage of a servant leader.

Now by our definition, Go to See also includes listening. Although we're using a different sense here to gather information, the biggest barrier we have to overcome is exactly the same—our assumptions.

We had a listening exercise we used to use at TMMK, and Ernie and I still use it in our sessions. Here's how it works: Divide the group into pairs. One person talks on a subject of his or her choice for two minutes, and the other listens. Then, the listener is asked to paraphrase what he or she heard to the satisfaction of the person who did the talking.

Guess what? 80 percent of the people do not meet the expectations of the test. And the reason is that the "listeners" are busy making assumptions about how they are going to paraphrase, and are not really opening their ears fully to what the other person is saying.

The instruction to "just listen" is very difficult to follow if making assumptions is your "go to" strategy for dealing with reality. This is something we have to work hard on every day. And the moment you think you've finally "got it," you can be sure that there's a deeper lesson to be learned.

GOING TO SEE AT RELIABLE

After their initial meeting, Clayton and Brody-san completed many *gemba* walks at Reliable. Brody-san said very little. Often he would just stand and watch, calmly, but very intently. Sometimes he took interest in what was posted on the visual charts. He frequently asked workers why they were doing something, but he always showed genuine interest rather than sounding critical. Sometimes, he asked questions that didn't seem to be directly related to their work. Clayton noticed that Brody-san showed enormous respect for the workers, as if they were the leaders.

After a few days, the two got together in Clayton's office. Clayton was very impatient to move forward, and he had prepared a list of problems with Reliable's culture.

"Tell me, Brody-san," he asked, "now that you have seen my *gemba* and talked to my people, what is wrong with our culture?"

"There are many problems with your culture," he said. "It would take a great deal of time to solve them all. Even Toyota is still improving its culture after working on it for 60 years."

"Then please tell me what my biggest problems are," said Clayton. "I understand that improvement will mean an investment of time and resources, but at least we can get started."

"Unless you can see these problems yourself, I can't help you," said Brody-san. "You have seen everything I have seen, and much more."

Clayton was silent for a moment. Then Brody-san suddenly asked, "What is your purpose as vice president of manufacturing?"

Clayton had a strong sense of the company's True North. "My purpose is to develop my people so that we can build safe, reliable, energy-efficient cars that are a joy to own," he said almost automatically.

"That's where you'll find your answer," said Brody-san.

Clayton's learning journey, however, was only just beginning, as we will see in the next chapter.

6

Grasp the Situation

■ ■ ■

There is a saying that a problem clearly defined is a problem half solved. Of course, this begs a very important question—what do we mean when we say that a problem is clearly defined? At TMMK, this question was never left to our instincts—we had strict standards for how we defined problems, and like Go to See, there was a lot of situational learning and coaching from our trainers to help us deepen our thinking and grow our abilities in this critical area. "Tracey-san," they would often say, "please grasp the situation."

Like Go to See, Grasp the Situation is a way of thinking that goes on constantly. However, it becomes particularly critical when a person is in the "P" stage of PDCA (Plan, Do, Check, Act), that is, planning to make a change to a process. Similarly, Grasp the Situation determines much of the thinking behind the first three steps in Toyota's eight-step problem-solving process:

1. Clarify the problem
2. Break down the problem
3. Target setting

Grasp the Situation is about making sure that you not only define and frame a problem correctly, but remain ever wary of the natural human tendency to look at problems superficially and then "countermeasure" them before they are clearly defined.

Jumping to conclusions here is not only wasteful activity, but can lead to "solutions" that create more harm than good, and are also very discouraging to a workforce and its culture.

Unfortunately, very few organizations even recognize this as a problem. Managers tend to go with their intuitions or tribal knowledge and don't take the time fully to Grasp the Situation, resulting in "firefighting" situations when their assumptions don't pan out. In fact, if a manager does try to Grasp the Situation, he or she might be accused of being too hesitant or indecisive. "Don't waste your time on that," a superior might say, "just do whatever it takes to get those results."

As with many aspects of our work at TMMK, Grasp the Situation calls for some very different thinking about how we work and manage, and it takes lots of daily practice and mental conditioning to become really proficient at it. And as you may have guessed, there is always room to improve and develop others in this way as we continue on our journey of "leading and learning."

During my early days at TMMK, I was on a pretty steep learning curve around this. I would spot an abnormality, and the problem would seem fairly apparent to me. So I would report to my trainer and say something like, "We've had a few situations . . . ," and he would stop me right there.

"Tracey-san," he would say politely, "I don't understand what you mean by 'a few,' can you please explain?"

"Oh, you know, *several*," I might have responded.

"I don't understand 'several,' can you please explain?" he would say. Now of course, he understood what the words meant—I remember a translator jokingly saying, "He will always say he doesn't understand until you stop using subjective words and start giving him facts."

The issue is that "a few" is likely to mean different things to different people, and my trainer didn't know for sure what "a few" meant to me or the company. In other words, I wasn't being specific enough to approach the problem in a manner that could lead to a predictable and sustainable solution. To do that, I needed to measure the data to get the facts.

The idea of solving problems and making improvements at TMMK had a lot to do with standards, and we'll discuss the various nuances of this in the chapter on Get to Standard. Let me just say for now that to us, a standard was *the best known method at the moment that meets the internal and external customer expectations, and which we all agree to follow with accountability until we improve it.* In order to maintain that consensus, we need to be sure that we are talking in precise terms so that everybody is on the same page.

So we became very wary of terms like "a few" or "several" and got used to quantifying the problem clearly and definitively so that any person who measured it in the same way would get the same results. This is essential to the methodical thinking that TMMK embedded in all of our work. It is also consistent with the scientific approach because it is very similar to what we might do in a lab—make a hypothesis, and then rigorously test it in order to prove definitively that it is either correct or incorrect.

COUNTERING OUR REACTIVE NATURE WITH ATAR

Jumping to conclusions and then acting prematurely is a pervasive habit that is wired into our brains, and very difficult to break. We often use the acronym ATAR to help learners visualize this. ATAR means we allow Assumptions to alter our Thinking, which can change the Action(s) we are about to take and skew Results (ATAR). If we remain vigilant that ATAR is always lurking underneath the surface, we can break this difficult habit over time.

WORKING WITH FACTS
INSTEAD OF ASSUMPTIONS

Grasp the Situation is particularly important when we first start to consider changing a process. Here, we begin by quantifying a particular problem so that we can create a definitive course of action. To do this, we frame the problem around three questions. For each situation, we ask:

1. What is the standard? (Or what should be happening?)
2. What is the current state?
3. What is the measurable gap?

When my trainers said, "Tracey-san, you must grasp the situation," as they often did, they were reminding me to frame the problem with these three questions in mind.

Let's look at an example of a real workplace problem with a company that we'll call Company X. Company X operates a clinic to provide medical services for employees, which they receive as part of their compensation package.

Management at Company X began to see evidence, perhaps from people in HR who had talked to their colleagues in other companies, that the costs of running the clinic were higher than they should have been.

Now, it would be typical for senior managers in this case to start looking right away at the largest cost items, and then ask process owners in these areas to make cuts. But in Company X, the leader who was responsible for the clinic understood the importance of Grasp the Situation.

They began this thinking with question 1—what should be the standard for medical costs? To determine this, they chose the average cost per patient visit, which correlates the costs of running the clinic with the value that customers, that is, employees who visit the clinic, receive. Looking at data from various health organizations, they determined that the national average was $72 per visit, based on a 20-minute appointment slot for each patient.

Next, they determined the current state by dividing the total cost of operating the clinic by the number of patient visits. The number they arrived at was $93 per visit.

This left a $21 gap between what that per-visit cost was and what it should have been. So, armed with this quantifiable gap, the team had something real and substantial to work on.

Now, there are several very important considerations here. First of all, imagine what would happen if we reacted based on an assumption or "tribal knowledge." What if we got careless and misread that data, and the gap we detected was much larger or much smaller than it actually was? In that case, we might quickly venture off in the wrong direction, wasting resources and potentially damaging medical services to our employees in the process. So it's extremely important to do this first step carefully and thoroughly.

Secondly, we are surmising that if our costs are much higher than everybody else's, there must be waste in the process. It must be very clear that in making these improvements, we're not looking for cuts—we're using Go to See to find waste. This is very different from the mindset that we are going to cut costs regardless of the impact on customers.

Another consideration is whether the problem is significant enough to justify action. A gap of $21 per visit is substantial, and when you multiply that by thousands of visits, you're going to see a sizeable impact on the bottom line for the company.

But if the gap is much smaller, say a dollar or two, we should probably be looking for larger problems to work on, that is, problems where we could make a greater impact according to the company's key performance indicators (KPIs) and True North.

At the same time, we need to remain conscious of what is appropriate for us take on given our level and job scope. When we get engaged in projects or problems that involve a variety of people and resources, it's easy to fall into the "scope creep" trap where we get drawn into areas outside of our responsibility, and then find ourselves in over our heads. When deciding what we are going to work on, therefore, we should keep in mind that our problem-solving work should always connect to the larger strategy in the organization, which is based on everybody contributing at their particular level. We'll talk more about these linkages in Part 3.

Now, the problem with the clinic is straightforward in one respect—it is easy to quantify because the costs are clearly defined. In other cases, defining the gap is more difficult—perhaps you are trying to improve morale, or customer satisfaction, or some other "soft" indicator like employee engagement. Many managers would reject the idea of trying to assign a number to these.

Here's a challenge from a participant, who works in the financial sector, in a past workshop:

> I believe we need to work as well with qualitative measures, rather than trying to boil everything down to quantifiable. In our world, you're going to have teams who are going to tune off to the idea of assigning numbers to everything. We have, for example, a framework for measuring our executives' engagement with our major clients. There are some links to our loan activity, but there are no numbers to go with a lot of the indicators that we are tracking. Of course, you have to always have measurements. But not all of them are going to have numbers.

We explained to the group that these "soft" measurements give the impression that we are measuring and improving, but they are not verifiable, and consequently, can't be relied on to produce sustainable results. If a measurement doesn't have a number, how do you know for sure that you've met your target? And how could you know that Manager A and Manager B would assess how well the said executive was engaging with major clients in a fair, unbiased, and consistent way? The fact is, you couldn't.

The issue here is that many people are in the habit of framing the discussion around the outcome—"engaged people"—as opposed to the problem that needs to be solved. A statement like "our executives aren't engaged enough" isn't really a defined problem, and therefore should never be our starting point. What we need are specifics that we can act on. So we need to determine how lack of engagement is a problem, what discrepancies we are seeing because a person isn't engaged, how we can measure that, and how we will know if we've been successful at correcting the problem.

To uncover this, we often start with a series of questions. What does an engaged person look like? How do we know when people are truly engaged? When a person is engaged, what tangible actions can we expect to see? What is the measure? Then we need to ask "why?" until we get a clear understanding of how poor executive engagement is affecting the company. It could ultimately lead to higher-than-normal customer turnover, for example, or perhaps an inordinate number of failed financial products. But if we don't ask "why" and get down to a quantifiable gap that needs to be solved, we are fooling ourselves if we think we're going to make substantial improvements. That is, unless we happen to get lucky, which, as we said earlier, is not a sustainable strategy. (If luck were really sustainable, the casino industry would be out of business!)

This also brings us back to a point we mentioned in Go to See—the line of sight to the True North. At TMMK, we all knew how our work contributed to the purpose of the company, and we built on that every day. So if something like engaging with major clients comes up, the purpose behind it should be obvious. At TMMK, we knew we were on to something when we visualized the connection to the most critical KPIs for the company. We also knew which problems to prioritize based on our KPIs.

CLAYTON CONNECTS WITH
HIS TRUE NORTH

After Brody-san had challenged him to identify what was wrong with the company's culture, Clayton spent some time thinking about the events of the past few days. Brody-san had only spent a short time at Reliable, but he seemed to see everything, almost as if he had x-ray vision. Yet Clayton knew that he himself had seen everything that Brody-san had seen—the difference was the thinking.

At their next meeting, Clayton's list of problems had grown larger, and was now so large that he felt overwhelmed.

"I've thought about our True North," he said, "but clearly I don't have a deep enough understanding to take the right step. Please help me understand better."

Brody-san sat quietly for a moment. Then he asked, "What is your most important program for developing people?"

Now Clayton knew that the most successful program for developing people at Reliable was its Quality Circle program. In fact, many of the leaders in the company had discovered their leadership talents through Quality Circles. Clayton also remembered that participation in Quality Circles, which was voluntary, had declined recently.

"I've got it!" he said. "To improve our culture, we must have better Quality Circle participation."

This time, Brody-san gave a puzzled look. "I have no idea what you mean by better," he said.

Clayton thought for a minute. "Well," he said at last, "if we want to improve our culture we must increase the Quality Circle participation levels."

"Very good," said Brody-san. "Now we must lay out the facts in order to understand the problem clearly."

Now, Clayton had taken a course in A3 and knew how to follow the eight steps of the Toyota Business Practices. Clayton spoke to Bob, his Lean coordinator, and together they gathered

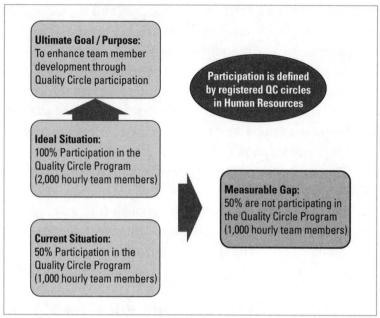

FIGURE 6.1 Step 1: Clarify the Problem

statistics on the QC program over the past few years to differentiate between what should be happening (ideal state) and what
was actually happening (current state).

The next day when Brody-san came in, Clayton was very
excited. Clayton went to the whiteboard and drew the diagram
shown in Figure 6.1. "Yes, there is clearly a measurable gap
here," said Brody-san, "and you have clarified a problem that
aligns with the top priorities of your company with respect to
your ultimate goal. Now you can enter that into your A3 under
Step 1: Clarify the Problem."

Clayton was excited to have reached this milestone. "Our
organization is very excited about Lean, and can create a great
awareness campaign to get better participation," he said. "Now
we know exactly what gap we are trying to close."

Brody-san was used to people jumping to solutions. "What
proof do you have that an awareness campaign would work?"

he asked. "If you go to a solution like that, you are relying on luck, and luck is not a strategy. We can only be sure of solving our gap if we base our inquiry on facts."

"That's why Toyota developed the eight-step process," he continued. "You must always follow the process in the correct order, never allow yourself to move faster than the facts you confirm at the *gemba*, and never let down your guard against the dangers of assumptions."

"Very well," said Clayton impatiently. "What is the next step?"

"We need to break down this problem into manageable pieces, by using the four *W* questions—what, where, when, and who. That way we will find the point of occurrence."

THE FINE ART OF ASKING QUESTIONS

As we move forward in our efforts to Grasp the Situation, much of the information we gather will be acquired by asking questions of people who work daily with the processes we are trying to improve, and who know a lot more about these processes than we do. How we ask, however, has a major impact on the quantity and quality of the information we receive.

What we want to avoid, essentially, is turning the questioning process into some kind of interrogation. Ernie and I teach a module on this, and essentially, it's all about reversing the words *you* and *I*. For example, if I walk up to Ernie and say, "Ernie, why did you do that?" I'm already insinuating that he did something wrong. In response, he could already be on the defensive before we've even begun our discussion. I also have to keep in mind that many people have different communication styles from me, and might respond differently than I would.

So I might get an answer like, "Well, Tracey, why did you design this inefficient process?" And then we start going back and forth, getting nowhere.

Reversing the *you* and the *I* changes the dynamic. I might say, "Ernie. How are you doing? I need your help on this process. You're the professional on this process and know all the knacks and feels. You do this every single day."

I could then go further. "Do you mind walking me through what steps you take so I can have a better understanding?" This way I am more apt to grasp the nuances of the process, and utilize that "go to see" moment with the process owner. What I'm consciously doing is shifting the responsibility, and any possible blame, to myself as the leader in order to remove the barriers and constraints for the process owner to be successful. Furthermore, I am showing that I respect what the process owner knows, and what that person's opinions are about the situation.

Once the trust has been created, and the experts are freely sharing their knowledge, you can begin to ask more questions, as you will have to do in the A3 process. Undoubtedly you will already have some of the answers after the employee has shared his or her views, but there will always be more.

All these questions will help us create an accurate picture of the quantitative facts regarding the standard, the current state, and the measurable gap. Once we have done this, we have clarified the problem, and come a long way from running to our trainer or leader and saying, "I know there's a problem because I've seen a few cases where . . ." Now, we have the information needed to decide if further steps are justified, whether we will make that decision on our own or in consultation with our leader.

SEEING PROBLEMS IN A NEW LIGHT

Al Mason, Vice President, Operational Excellence, Altra Industrial Motion

There are two tendencies in the way people deal with problems. First, there's this pressure to jump to answers right away without getting the facts. The other is that people want to "solve world hunger" by taking on a huge complex problem all at once.

We had a business unit trying to figure out why its deliveries were late about half the time. This was a big problem, so the management team got together for a brainstorming session, complete with an outside facilitator. Many ideas were tabled and discussed, and they had a wall full of sticky notes.

However, when I later asked whether they had gone to see the situation, and whether they had gathered any facts through direct observation, they said no. Instead, they told me about how well the brainstorming session had gone, and how thorough that process was. So they were feeling pretty confident, but they had no idea what the root causes of the problem were.

BREAKING DOWN THE PROBLEM

If we have correctly identified a quantifiable gap, we are one step closer to fully Grasping the Situation. We now have a clear understanding that there is a measurable discrepancy that is preventing us from meeting a particular expectation in the process. It could be waste. It could be rework. It could be that we don't have all the resources we need. But until we investigate further, we won't know, and are therefore in no position to start planning a solution. And once again, we must guard against the temptation to choose assumptions over facts.

Thinking ahead, we're going to have to come up with a practical solution, that is, a series of actions we can implement with available resources that will cause a minimum of disruption to the existing work environment. So before we even contemplate chasing root causes, we have to direct our inquiry appropriately.

One of the big challenges here is the tendency, which is encouraged in many management cultures, to take on complex, large-scale "world hunger" problems all at once. When some managers first discover the A3 approach, they see this as a magic shortcut for solving such problems more quickly. Even in my time at TMMK, I caught myself being pulled into this vortex.

To illustrate the dangers here, I like to use the iceberg analogy. When we're staring at a quantified gap, we may not see the many interconnected factors that might be influencing it, that is, the larger portion of the proverbial iceberg looming under the surface. And if we move in and start acting on that problem without proper knowledge of all of the implications, we could be creating a dangerous situation for ourselves and the company.

The difficulty is that if we introduce too many countermeasures to a process at the same time, we can never learn which countermeasures worked, which didn't, and which are actually harmful. We could also be creating a lot of disruption in our process, and those that are affected by it.

This is similar to what happens when we are sick with a cold or flu, and our doctor prescribes several medications. Some medications may not agree with us. If we took them all at once, we wouldn't know which one made us feel bad, and we could be endangering our health. Therefore, our doctor might direct us to take them several hours apart to determine the best medication and avoid harmful side effects.

When I first was introduced to problem solving, I will admit we often went from a larger measurable gap to asking "why," usually with the help of a fishbone diagram. This process often yielded more root causes than we could handle at one time. Many times we found ourselves firefighting outside of the *gemba* as we tried to make the best selection based on assumptions, opinions, and past experiences.

This may not sound so bad on the surface, especially if the people involved know their area very well, but it's not a sustainable process—lucky at best, as my trainers would remind me. It's much more efficient in the long run if we approach this methodically in order to ensure that we're on track as we go.

That way, we avoid rework and non-value added time. As John Wooden said, "If you don't have time to do it right, when will you have time to do it over?"

Breaking down a problem into manageable pieces is a little like slicing a pizza before eating it, and that's the analogy we like to use in our sessions. If we tried to take on a pizza all at once without it being sliced, eating it would probably be a messy operation, and we might not feel very well afterward. So slicing the pizza first has become the preferred method, and if we attack problems in the same way, we'll find that we can move toward a sustainable solution.

In problem solving, our entire quantified gap is like the whole pizza. We begin by slicing the gap into manageable pieces that are of reasonable scope for us to handle given our capabilities, resources, and responsibilities. We then prioritize these according to their anticipated KPI impact on our gap.

Next, we select the slice that we expect will have the most impact, and designate this as our prioritized problem (PP). Once we have solved the prioritized problem and verified through our data at the *gemba* that we have successfully removed that portion of the gap, we repeat the process with another slice, and so on, until the gap is gone.

One of the questions we are often asked is how large to make the slices. There is no hard-and-fast rule here, but the best indicator is the number of root causes. Two to three are common and manageable, but if we find that there are more than five, that's a red flag that we need to consider breaking down the problem further.

Also, we may not know about many of the root causes until later in the problem-solving process. This is one of many possible reasons why we may have to go back and revise our plan based on the information that was gathered during the process. If we find that the slice was too big, we may have to narrow it down later on. This was considered part of the learning process, and never viewed as a sign of failure.

Another consideration when choosing our "slice" is that there may be "micro" processes within the "macro" process we are looking at. For example, if I were to explain the process of my "morning routines," the flow of events might look like this:

Get up >> Get ready >> Eat breakfast >> Drive to work

This might seem like a pretty reasonable sequence of steps at a first glance. But if I start to see multiple points of occurrence in a single step, I may not have broken it down far enough. In that case, it may be more manageable if I break down "Get ready" as follows:

Take shower >> Dry hair >> Put on makeup >> Get dressed

Looking for the "micros" within the "macro" can help you determine when you've broken down the problem sufficiently, that is, to the extent where you have no more than two or three root causes to address in root cause analysis. It also helps you see the relationship between the overall "mother gap" and all the "child gaps" that it will spawn in the breakdown. By implementing a series of "child A3s" to close these "child gaps," we effectively and efficiently eliminate the overall gap "a slice at a time."

The need to break down problems becomes even more pronounced in a large organization, where a major gap can be the result of hundreds or even thousands of contributing factors. Solving a measured quality gap in a particular model of car, for example, might involve a large series of projects throughout the organization. By breaking down the problem through an interconnected series of A3s, leaders present their people with problems that can be addressed at their respective levels.

Figure 6.2 shows how my role as group leader in Plastics would be impacted by a major gap. Let's assume that leadership has challenged production to reduce the overall number of defects by 500. By looking at data showing where the defects are occurring in the organization, leaders at different levels would

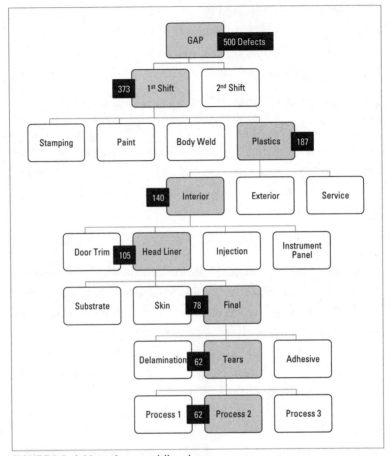

FIGURE 6.2 Addressing a multilevel gap

assign a smaller portion (a slice) to their people. In this case, I "owned" a 62-defect prioritized problem as my slice of closing that gap. I had to raise the bar, working with my people to understand our gap, find the root cause, test countermeasures, and improve our standards.

As a group leader in Plastics, I got very good at solving problems in that area and, through that, was able to help our senior managers move the needle forward on their most critical KPIs, and in the direction of True North. I would, in turn, break down the problems I was presented with further so that each of my team leaders and team members could understand the gap at their level and make a difference.

AN ENGINEER TACKLES COMPLEX PROBLEMS

Al Mason, Vice President, Operational Excellence, Altra Industrial Motion

I'm an engineer by training. I like complex situations, and I have a bias for grabbing onto difficult, multidimensional problems, and immediately trying to solve a bunch of simultaneous equations and get to the answer. Tracey and Ernie really helped me understand the importance of breaking down problems so that you can chip away at those underlying factors one by one, rather than changing 15 things at a time. We want to isolate our efforts to a critical few root causes so that we can set up structured experiments according to the PDCA process. And then we become real scientists.

Looking back, we used to just grab at a problem, and flail away at 15 or 20 variables using all kinds of Lean tools and statistical analysis techniques. Sometimes we'd have an impact, but we never knew which two or three countermeasures were the essential ones, and which dozen or so were a waste of time.

FINDING THE POINT OF OCCURRENCE

Once we've successfully broken down our overall problem into a set of smaller prioritized problems, and then selected the most appropriate slice of the gap to pursue, we need to turn to a new series of questions. Exactly where in the process does the discrepancy creating that portion of the gap reside? Can we recognize it? Do we consider it an accepted norm? Have we developed workarounds to embed it as part of our process? Does tribal knowledge cloud our thinking? Through asking these questions and observing at the *gemba*, we can start to isolate the problem down to a very specific process.

In our sessions, we jokingly ask, "Have you discovered the point of occurrence in your process(es)?" We often refer to it as the POO (point of occurrence). We say if you have "stepped in the POO," you have found the discrepancy that is creating "pain," from a KPI perspective, for your organization. The pain can be in the form of quality, safety, productivity, or cost. And this is the precise point where we need to act in order to eliminate the problem.

As you move closer to the problem, it's critical to maintain your awareness of the linkage between the gap and what is happening at that point of occurrence. Keep in mind the chain of events: identify the quantified gap—break the gap down into manageable slices—prioritize the slices by KPI or team member impact—select the first slice as the prioritized problem—determine, by engaging with the process owner(s) at the *gemba*, exactly where the point of occurrence resides.

Sometimes you will find that there is more than one point of occurrence. In this case, it's important to begin by working with the first one, that is, the one located earliest in the process. If there are too many points of occurrence, it may be necessary to go back and break down the problem further. The point is, our problem-solving process must never be allowed to get out of control.

In a complex manufacturing environment, it can be very difficult to determine exactly where a particular anomaly is happening. Here's a great example of that.

Tracking Down a Perplexing Problem

One day a team member at TMMK noticed an intermittent scratch occurring on one of the interior parts. The team member pulled the *andon* to alert the team leader, since it had occurred more than once. The team leader looked at the process carefully and confirmed that the scratch hadn't been created by equipment, another part, or a person. A deeper observation of the standard work and discussions with the team member failed to uncover any potential causes that could be recreated.

The vendor who provided the part was then asked to do a process confirmation to ensure that the defect wasn't occurring within its processes. The supervisor at the vendor did the same level of checks. (At TMMK, we worked with our vendors so that they followed the same approach to these situations as we did.)

After the vendor was unable to find any indication of the defect in its processes, the only logical conclusion was that the defect was occurring in the transportation of the parts from the vendor to TMMK. These particular parts were being shipped in truckloads (each truck was considered a *kanban*) of approximately 80 sets, that is, the number of sets needed for 80 cars.

To find out where in the transportation process the defects occurred, the team decided to have somebody "ride" with the parts. They designed a safe way for the supervisor to sit in the back of the truck during the entire trip and equipped that person with a radio to pass on observations as they occurred.

The first ride yielded no clues as to where the problem was occurring. The parts went in without a scratch, and came off the truck without any. The same occurred the next day, and after several days of this, it was becoming more and more a mystery as to why this was happening.

Then, a few days later, the defect appeared again. Each side did their confirmations as before, and were honestly becoming a little frustrated. How could they ever get to the root cause of this intermittent problem? They decided that they would take another ride with the parts to just be sure there wasn't something they had missed on the previous observations.

As the supervisor boarded the truck along with the parts, he strapped in for the ride with eyes wide open. On this particular journey, something happened that hadn't happened the other ride-alongs. About halfway between the two facilities, there was a jolt as if the truck had hit a large bump in the road. Most trucks aren't equipped with the kind of shock absorption you get in a passenger car, so it gave a little "jump" to all the parts in the truck. The parts were suddenly lifted by about four to five inches, and then came crashing down.

The supervisor radioed the driver and asked, "Did you hit something? We had a good bounce back here!"

The driver said, "No, I didn't see anything."

But then he added, "Usually I have to stop at the light here because this is a very busy intersection, but this time I made the light. There's an indentation in the road just past the light, but we only get a bounce from it when we make the light and are driving at our normal speed."

After a few questions, the supervisor determined that the driver made the light 10 to 15 percent of the time, and the bounce had occurred when the truck was traveling at the speed limit of 35 mph.

So the point of occurrence was identified as the back of the truck at the point where it crossed that particular indentation in the road, but only when the truck made the light and was traveling at 35 mph.

This led to more precise observations. There were parts of the truck van that were more affected than others, and it turned out that the defects were coming from parts at the rear end of the truck that were at the bottom of their particular stack. It also turned out that some were covered with plastic foam better than others.

So as you can see, the point of occurrence can be very elusive, and it can take a lot of observation, grasping the situation, and open discussion to uncover it.

ZEROING IN ON THE PRIORITIZED PROBLEM

After the last meeting with Brody-san, Clayton asked HR to compile data on Quality Circle participation over the past year, sorted by department. To show the data in context, they created the diagram shown in Figure 6.3.

Clearly, Assembly 1 Trim section had by far the highest number of incomplete themes (150). But Clayton was far too wise to assign blame. He knew that his people wanted to do the right thing for the company, and if there was something lacking, it was a discrepancy in the process.

"We must Go to See, and find out more about the process for Quality Circles in Assembly 1," said Brody-san. "If we look carefully at the facts, we will find the problem."

After going to the process to look deeper at the situation, they sat down to discuss the matter with Ashley, the group leader for the area, and several others. "The breakdown shows us that the number of incomplete themes is 15 percent of the overall gap," said Brody-san. "We will now identify this number as your prioritized problem."

Once again, Clayton felt they had "arrived" and was eager to jump to a solution. But once again, Brody-san urged him to resist the temptation to get ahead of the data.

"First you need to map out what the process of the prioritized problem is and what should be happening," said Brody-san. "Otherwise, how do we know how improving the number of theme completions is going to help us?"

Clayton asked Ashley to map out the ideal process for Quality Circles. Ashley went up to the whiteboard and made the diagram shown in Figure 6.4, highlighting the point where the irregularity was occurring.

The diagram showed how the discrepancy was occurring at the point where a team member was interested in completing a QC theme, but had not taken action. It was easy to see how this

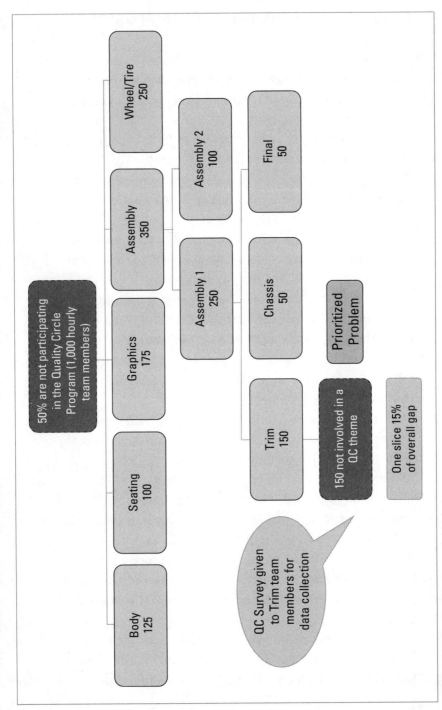

FIGURE 6.3 Quality Circle participation

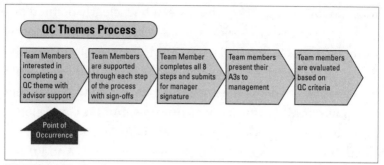

FIGURE 6.4 Point of occurrence

was disrupting the entire process. Nothing was even getting off the ground, and problems weren't even being reported.

"This is our point of occurrence," said Brody-san, "and this is where we will now focus our efforts. Now that we understand the point of occurrence and the impact that this discrepancy is having, it's time to make a commitment to correct the problem."

COMMITTING TO ACTION

As we have seen, Grasp the Situation is all about understanding both sides of our gap—what the situation is, and what it should be. In the final stage of Grasp the Situation, we make a practical determination of the results we can expect to accomplish when pursuing a solution, and then set a target accordingly.

Targets in the eight-step process pertain specifically to the prioritized problem at the point of occurrence. Sometimes people make the mistake of setting a target to the overall gap, which defeats the purpose of all the work we did to break down the problem. We want very specific, achievable, measurable targets here so that we can pursue them through a disciplined and completely transparent process.

This doesn't mean, however, that targets should be easy. Thanks to motivational speakers like Zig Ziglar and Brian Tracy, most people in business are aware of how clearly defined targets can inspire us to perform at our very best. To give a sports example, it's like a football team setting a target of winning the Super Bowl. You don't know how you're going to do it, or what obstacles you're going to encounter, but you set that goal, and that governs all of your actions. Injuries, fumbles, and stellar performances from the opposing defense might get in the way, but that doesn't stop you from setting that target. And I think most people would agree that the players will be a lot more motivated about trying to win the Super Bowl, even if the prospects are uncertain, then they would about simply trying to "do as well as we can."

Toyota took this thinking a step further. First of all, the idea of ownership was very clear. As we discussed earlier, Toyota employees have a very strong line of sight, where they are aware of exactly how their work supports a large-scale team effort to achieve the company's objectives and to help the customer have a smile. So targets were very personal—if the improvement was within the scope of a process that you owned, you took ownership, and that was ingrained in the culture from the day we started with the company.

Personal development was also on everybody's mind when targets were considered. As you will remember, we spent one half of our time as leaders developing our people. Therefore, we always encouraged our people to set targets that not only maximized the chances of a successful project, but ensured that the project would create the best personal development opportunities.

This defies the conventional logic that it's best to pursue "safe" targets that are a sure bet. For example, let's say you're an employee starting a project, and your gap calls for a 50 percent improvement. You're not sure you can do that, but you figure you'll have no problem with 20 percent, so you put that on your A3. This way you'll make sure that you look good to management after the whole thing is done.

This would never be an acceptable way of thinking at TMMK. If you presented an unambitious target like this, trainers would say, "This is too easy. Targets are meant to be very challenging not only for you an as individual, but for the organization collectively. I want to see your thinking behind the process, based on what is actually attainable when resources are put toward the target."

Their concern is not that they want more work out of you. It is that they want you to develop as a problem solver. They want to see deeper thinking, observations, and greater confidence in your abilities, and they know that it's only possible to do that if, you guessed it, you step outside of your comfort zone.

Now don't get me wrong. They weren't trying to set us up for failure every time. In fact, the whole idea of breaking down the problem, as we saw earlier, was to provide a realistic opportunity for success. But they did want us to have the experience of pursuing challenging targets and trying things we'd never tried before, and there's always going to be some risk associated with that. Their respect of our ability to find our way, and their understanding that mistakes are part of the learning process, gave us the "space to think" and the opportunity to build experiences from our trials and tribulations.

NOT ENOUGH CHALLENGE

**Russ Scaffede, former Vice President
and General Manager, Powertrain,
Toyota Motor Manufacturing Kentucky**

One day Mr. Cho came over to my area and said, "Russ-san, the executive coordinators have been talking, and we're concerned that maybe you're not challenging the team enough. We see that you have not shut the vehicle plant down yet by driving your team to make continuous improvement."

> Now, at the time, it was only two or three years since my General Motors days.
>
> "Mr. Cho, you don't understand," I said, "that's career threatening. You lose your job at GM if you start shutting vehicle plants down."
>
> He said, "No, no. No problem. If you're challenging your team very hard and you interrupt the vehicle plant a little bit, no problem. Just don't do the same problem twice."

Another important aspect is that targets sometimes have to be changed. Many unexpected events can crop up during an improvement project. We might discover, for example, a series of root causes that weren't apparent on the surface, or we might find that in implementing an improvement, we are creating unsuspected difficulties for some of our neighboring processes.

Sometimes, we might find it more productive to set a series of interim targets in order to achieve our goal. This gives the process owner a sense of moving the needle, and also helps to adjust the final target based on information that is gathered along the way.

The point is, revising a plan later on was never seen as a setback or a source of blame. If anything, it may have been a sign that we had challenged ourselves a bit too much. As long as we kept learning, this was not a bad thing.

CLAYTON ARRIVES AT A TARGET

Clayton had learned all about target setting in business school. The philosophy he had been taught was that targets should always be doable, so that people could be sure of success without demanding too much out of people. He explained this to Brody-san, suggesting that doubling the number of completed themes, from 20 to 40, in Assembly would be a reasonable target.

Brody-san sat quietly for a moment. "Is doubling that number going to make a significant contribution to solving your overall gap?" he asked.

Clayton thought for a moment, and then admitted that it would hardly make a dent.

"Then we must select a target that addresses the problem at the point of occurrence to the extent where it will narrow the gap in a meaningful and visible way. Otherwise, how will we know if our efforts to solve the problem are successful? What would it take to close the gap completely for this prioritized problem?"

Clayton scribbled some numbers on a pad. "We'd have to increase from 20 completed themes to 150," he said. "I don't think my people could achieve that."

"Well, if the target turns out to be too high, what would you have to do?" asked Brody-san.

"We'd have to go back and change it, I guess," said Clayton. "But everyone would think we had failed."

"Why is adjusting your plan a failure?" asked Brody-san. "This is normal in a continuous improvement environment."

"150 completed themes is pretty extreme, though," said Clayton. "If I suggest something like that, I'm afraid people will get frustrated or overwhelmed."

Brody-san was silent for a minute. Then he suddenly asked, "What is preventing your people in assembly from completing 150 themes?"

Clayton was puzzled.

"Is it because your people are not interested, or don't care?" Brody-san asked.

"No," said Clayton. "I'm not blaming my people . . ." Then suddenly, a light bulb went on.

"Right," he said. "It's the process. If we improve the process, our people may be able to complete 150 themes without creating overburden or stress."

"Good," said Brody-san. "And remember that you have to continue to develop your people past what they think their capabilities are."

Clayton agreed that the target would be to increase the interest for raising theme completions to 150 in Assembly Trim 1 by March.

"Okay," said Clayton. "Now that we have set our target at the point of occurrence and have completed step 3, let's improve this broken process."

"First, we must find the root cause," said Brody-san.

Nailing down that root cause, as we'll see in the next chapter, was the team's first step in finding a sustainable solution to the problem.

7

Get to Solution

■ ■ ■

As we've shown earlier, our work processes at TMMK were constantly changing. When we'd visit an area of the plant that we hadn't seen for a while, we'd often notice that some of the processes were significantly different, even after only a few weeks.

Change, however, was never dictated by higher levels of management, but always achieved through consultation and consensus. There were no shortcuts. As a result, when we made a change to a process, we were usually successful in achieving the expected benefits. The magic ingredient for our success was—you guessed it—people!

Change management guru John Kotter clearly understood this when he said, "The central issue is never strategy, structure, culture, or systems. The core of the matter is always about changing the behavior of people."

Toyota never left the people factor to chance. Get to Solution is our term for the thinking behind making changes in a methodical way while involving people at every stage. Whether we changed a standard, tested a process improvement, or made adjustments to a process to accommodate a model change, we were always following the basic Get to Solution thinking.

Of course, we don't practice Get to Solution unprepared. Going to workers and talking about solutions without having reflected through Go to See and Grasp the Situation would be a show of disrespect. Before we demand people's time and attention, we need to be reasonably sure that their participation is going to be worth their time and effort.

Get to Solution thinking begins when we closely examine the point of occurrence at the process (narrowly focused from our selected "slice"—the prioritized problem) and repeatedly ask "why" until we determine the root cause. This activity marks a departure from previous problem-solving activities in that here, we need to consult intensively with the people directly involved at the process in order to confirm that our conclusions are correct. The idea is that unless we get their buy-in of what the root cause is, and have shown that we can recreate the problem at the *gemba*, it will be very difficult to confirm that we have made the correct determination, and equally difficult to implement a solution, even if we are correct.

Get to Solution sets the stage to involve others in asking "why" at the point of occurrence in the process. Once consensus is achieved and the root cause is confirmed, we then expand that consensus as we design, test, implement, and document our solution that removes the root cause.

One of the misunderstandings we see in companies pursuing the Lean approach is that process owners are brought into the conversation once a Gantt chart has been created. This follows the traditional thinking that "consultation" is an add-on of sorts—a little like the icing on a cake.

At Toyota, consultation was woven into the process because we recognized that people and process are inseparable. If we would rush ahead and leave workers in the process out of the conversation, our trainers would say, "This is a failure. These people shouldn't just be discovering changes taking place at the countermeasure step. They need to join in our consensus about what the problem is and how we're measuring from the very beginning."

Consequently, we would go through the thinking and measurements that led us to determine the gap, leading up to how we had identified the point of occurrence, and the target we hoped to achieve. Then we would ask questions like, "What have you seen? Do you have any input? Can we Go to See together?"

Part of the reason for being very careful here is that when we move our spotlight to the point of occurrence at the process, things can get dicey. One can say that at this point, a lot of things are going to *look* like the root cause. So it is very easy and very tempting to get impatient and jump to conclusions at this stage.

For example, it may seem an absolute certainty that somebody has failed to follow standard work. However, until we consult with people in the process, we will never know for sure. We jokingly say in our training sessions that it's easy to take the "five who's and the root blame" approach. We also like to remind people that the phrase "hey, we've seen this before" is probably an assumption, not a fact.

The problem is, assumptions often result in non-value added time for the individual and the company. Furthermore, mutual trust and respect will quickly dissolve if the process owners see their leaders basing decisions solely on assumptions at the expense of people. So we must always continue to Grasp the Situation as we proceed with Get to Solution.

All this underlines why it's so important to follow the five whys and root cause approach. People sometimes ask if it always has to be five whys, and the answer is no—it could be a two, or it could be seven. The point is, the "five" maxim was used by our trainers so we'd always think past the first one or two, and always be alert to the possibility of an unexpected "why" that's not visible on the surface.

Of course, our inquiry may well lead to a person or people who are not following standardized work. This does not usually signify laziness or willful negligence—there may have been contributing factors such as poor documentation, insufficient resources, an inadequate audit process, or a lack of training. However, people are likely to feel defensive when their own processes are being put in question, and we need to exercise respect for people in order to gain their trust and avoid cover-ups. If people will not willingly reveal the truth to us, we will not be able to uncover it in many situations.

Furthermore, we'll have these same people working against us later on if we haven't involved them. They're likely to say, "Why should I change my process? The other people should have to change," or "Why do I have to do it this way, my way is effective?" or the all-time favorite, "We have always done it this way."

FACILITATING CHANGE

As you will remember, our "boot camp" for leading change was Quality Circles. This was where I began to get over my fear of presenting to groups and began to develop my skills of gathering consensus. This was supported by the prepromotion courses in meeting facilitation that I took prior to becoming a group leader.

In general, all employees at TMMK were conditioned to the thinking behind asking questions in order to gain consensus. One of the main ideas is that you don't use a "majority rules" approach where the minority doesn't get a proper ear—it might be accurate to say that a "no idea is left behind" ethic applies. With a system that relies on each individual to follow the True North, it's not hard to understand why this approach was so important.

Let's look at a simple illustration of how all this plays out when we work together with the people in the process to determine a root cause. Let's take a familiar situation:

- Problem: I was late for work.
- Why? I was unable to get to work on time.
- Why? My car wouldn't start.
- Why? The battery was dead.
- Why? The battery lost its charge.
- Why? The alternator wasn't maintaining the battery's charge.
- Why? The alternator belt was broken.
- Why? The alternator belt had worn.
- Why? The maintenance schedule wasn't followed properly for belt replacement.

There are a couple of key points to remember here. First of all, we're not just trying to get the car going again—we're trying to find a way to make sure the incident never happens again. So it's not enough to simply replace the battery, which might be the first reaction, or to replace the alternator belt and get on with things.

To get to the root cause, we're going to have to gather some information from the process owners, who might see any question at all as assignment of blame, or who might not have a clear understanding of the process involved. Getting your mechanic or car dealer to admit that he or she didn't follow the maintenance schedule would require a lot of trust, and perhaps, it might ask them to expand their own way of thinking.

Now here's another challenge. In asking these whys, you are likely to confront a number of plausible possibilities—possibilities that might or might not be apparent to somebody with limited knowledge. In fact, each possible cause you identify might in turn have several other causes. The chain of thinking might follow a flow chart like the one in Figure 7.1.

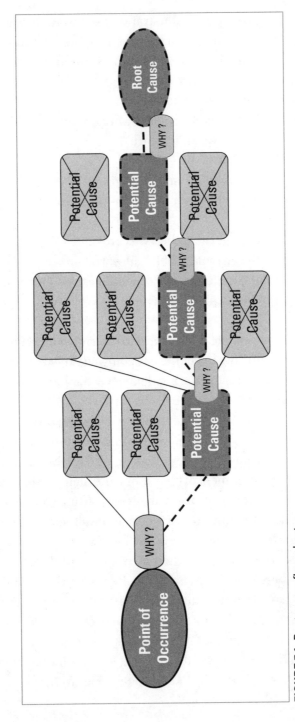

FIGURE 7.1 Root cause flow chart

In many cases, therefore, it's going take some local knowledge from the point of occurrence to sort these out. In the case of the car, few of us are able to diagnose whether we have a defective battery, a wiring problem, a defective alternator, or a broken alternator belt when we open the hood. So once again, we have to go to the process to ask people who know, and if we want our solution to be sustainable, we need their buy-in.

GETTING TO THE ROOT CAUSE

Alan Kandel, Global Head of Methods and Tools, Multinational Chemical Company

One of our company's primary values is to strive toward being leaders in sustainability. As such, we are always trying to improve our water usage, whether that's through recycling, reduction, or continuous improvement efforts. Obviously, to improve anything, you have to be able to measure it. One of our plant managers worked on a water reduction project. His plant measured water usage at a single location in the plant, the main water meter. This made it very difficult to understand where within the plant the main water usage took place. They decided to go through the painstaking process of tracing and measuring water usage at critical points and departments within the plant. By doing this they were able to break down the problem and follow the problem-solving process. What this plant manager ultimately found was that a lot of water was being lost due to a broken valve. This was not something easily noticeable in a remote part of the large facility.

So, his reaction was, "I've found the broken valve and we replaced it. No more major water losses. Problem solved, right?" It took a little bit of convincing to make him understand that the valve was not the true root cause. To prevent the problem from ever happening again, we have to get to the true root cause by asking, "Why did the valve break?" We had to coach him to continue with the thinking process by moving forward through the methodology, pointing out that if you just replace the valve, the problem is going to come back at some point in the future. Ultimately, the root cause was discovered to be the preventive maintenance schedule as well as the water usage measurement system. By understanding these two root causes, the plant was able to come up with a solution to ensure that the valve would never break again.

The light bulb that went off in this person's mind was, "Wow, you know, I wasn't really solving problems—I was sort of patching them." That level of realization comes to many when they truly work through this type of methodology. This is what Tracey and Ernie were trying to teach us from the very beginning, but until you experience it, it's very difficult to understand it.

In a factory like Toyota, determining a root cause can be quite complex. The root cause and the symptom, for example, might be linked through a significant chain of events. In such situations, it's important to never lose the context. Normally that's determined by KPI impact, or "pain to the organization," or it could be an immediate safety issue that overrides all else. Whatever the case, it must be clear why the organization is going to benefit from us solving this problem.

What Ernie and I have found over our years of experience in determining the root cause is that they fall into three categories:

- Lack of a standard or process
- Not following a standard
- Wrong or invalid standard

So I would say it's very difficult to get to the root cause without understanding the process involved. It's best if we can determine it from standardized work, but if there isn't documentation available then we have to map it out—if someone is creating an output, product, or service, there is always a process behind it. It may turn out that this process isn't consistently repeatable by all process owners, but by involving and engaging everyone in a mutual learning process, we can arrive at an appropriate documented standard that everyone can follow with accountability until that standard is improved.

A NEW WAY OF THINKING

Paul Trahan, Director of Customer Quality, Multinational Chemical Company

I think where we've seen the most impact is where we get people to understand that they have to avoid jumping to a solution, and to spend time on the planning part of the PDCA cycle so they get it right before they go further. It's really gratifying when somebody starts working on a problem this way and says, "Oh, wow! This is not where I expected to go with this." And the really great thing is that when people do this correctly, they get the satisfaction of knowing that they really solved the problem.

SORTING OUT THE WHITE SPACE

One of the most important challenges in finding the root cause is distinguishing between apparent root causes and real ones. If we Go to See, we will see many circumstances that appear to be connected, such as similar incidents occurring at a particular time of day, defects occurring when a particular team member is present, variations that appear to be influenced by changing environmental factors, or incidents that coincide with external (supplier/vendor) occurrences.

Consequently, when we ask "why" repeatedly in our efforts to find a root cause, we must pay particular attention to what I call the "white space" between the symptoms. This is where we believe the "cause and effect" relationship resides. Is there really a connection here, or does it just seem that way? We can test this by asking "why" as we move down the chain from effect to cause, and then double-check by saying "therefore" as we look upward from the suspected cause to the effect. Does this make sense both ways? We need to recognize our human tendency to connect the dots prematurely, make sure that we're absolutely sure before we move forward, and verify that every link in the "why" chain leading to the root cause is solid.

The biggest danger is that we wind up blaming people for a badly designed process. If, for example, we're looking at why a preventive maintenance program wasn't followed, many will be tempted to say, "Well, 'so and so' didn't follow the preventive maintenance because he was lazy." But this is an opinion, not a fact. But if we continue to ask why, we may learn that the instructions for a preventive maintenance procedure weren't given according to the standard, or training hadn't been adequate.

At Toyota, our thinking here was based on the idea that people want to do a good job, and will do so when given the opportunity. Automatically designating a person as the root cause in your A3 was considered not only disrespectful of people and ineffective, but unscientific. If in fact there was a personnel issue involved, it would be handled by human resources policy management, which had its own processes for corrective action. But this measure was taken only after we had thoroughly demonstrated that the process itself was not posing any barriers for the employees involved.

The big lesson here is that regardless of what we think a root cause might be, the only definitive test is being able to turn the symptom off and on by removing and then reapplying the condition that we have identified as the root cause.

MULTIPLE ROOT CAUSES

As we go through the steps of finding the root cause, there is no guarantee that there will be just one, and in a complex environment, there might be many. For example, a material shortage and transportation problems could both be contributing to late deliveries, and there could be even dozens of additional issues, such as staffing problems, supplier issues, or pressure from customers to stretch delivery dates.

When we get into multiple root causes, we need to once again apply the pizza analogy. Just as we can't solve world hunger, we can't expect to remove more than five root causes in a single project. Too many root causes, or even two that are completely unrelated, are a sign that we may not have broken down the problem sufficiently so that all slices are manageable.

This means that you have to go back and rethink your earlier steps. In many companies, that would be seen as a failure or a setback. At Toyota, this was seen as just another step in the learning process. We were always conditioned to go back through the process steps to understand what could have been overlooked or not verified.

FINDING THE ROOT CAUSE AT RELIABLE

Clayton and Brody-san spent two more days in assembly, talking to people who had and had not completed QC theme reports. They looked at successful projects to see if there were any roadblocks that people had needed to overcome. They also looked at QC projects that had started, but not continued. This was difficult, since in some cases people didn't bother to save records of projects that had never gotten off the ground.

"It's important to document your progress and your failures along the way," said Brody-san. "These are some of your most valuable lessons, and we must always be ready to share them with others. Remember, the primary purpose of Quality Circles is to develop people. How can you develop people if you throw out all of your lessons?"

Clayton saw that here was another hidden problem with their culture, and wrote this down in his notebook.

As they continued to talk to people, they focused on four potential causes:

- Are the team members insufficiently trained in the QC process?
- Are team members insufficiently skilled to see abnormalities in their processes?
- Is there poor morale in assembly that makes people not want to participate?
- Is there insufficient support for people who see abnormalities and want to initiate a QC process?

After many conversations with people currently in the QC program and further confirmation with team members, it was generally agreed that insufficient support was the primary cause that was preventing more QC projects.

"Great," said Clayton. "Now we know that we need more support. I will hire more people immediately."

"Please be patient," said Brody-san. "We still don't know why people aren't getting the support they need, so we don't really know that hiring people is the right solution. We need to keep asking "why" until we find the answer."

Clayton asked Ashley to facilitate the inquiry. "Why," she asked the group, "do team members feel they get low support through the process?" Ashley kept asking "why" until the group traced the problem to a lack of resources—the department didn't have the resources and organization structure to support the QC Coordinator as a dedicated position.

Ashley went to the whiteboard and carefully mapped out the entire chain of logic that led to this conclusion (Figure 7.2).

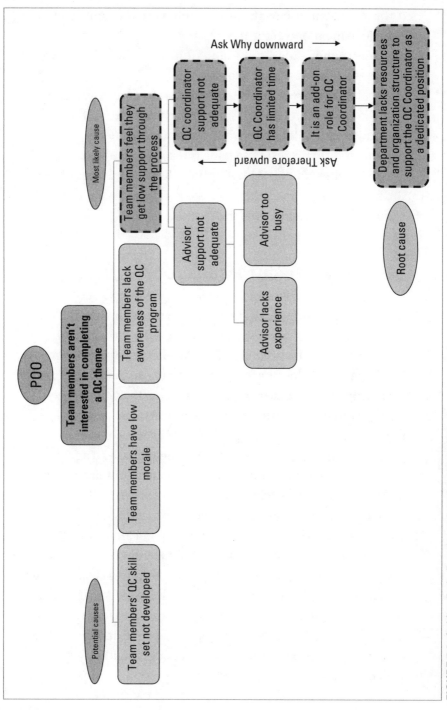

FIGURE 7.2 Asking "why" at the point of occurrence

It was clear that the next "why" would take the conversation outside of the scope of the project.

"Very good," said Brody-san. "This is our root cause. Now we are ready to plan countermeasures."

Lack of resources and organizational structure meant this was a larger problem than Clayton had expected, but he was determined. "I will meet with my management team, and we will make sure this resource issue is resolved," he said.

"You must consult with your people in the process," said Brody-san. "They own the process, and without their active support, your solution will fail."

MAPPING OUT A COURSE OF ACTION

As we see over and over again, the closer we get to the problem, the more tempting it is to say, "We've got the solution now. Let's just move forward." Anybody who finds the root cause correctly will have come a long way—from going to see the situation, to separating facts from assumptions, locating the point of occurrence, establishing a reasonable target, and finally, establishing the root cause. This sequence of thinking done correctly is a natural confidence booster that allows people to lead and learn more easily as they build their own problem-solving muscle and their ability to coach others.

However, once again, this is where we have to be patient and disciplined. Why? I think you know the answer already—people!

Toyota constantly reinforced the idea of starting on the people side of things before the results side, and to avoid saying things like "Let's hurry up and get this done—who cares what people think?" Once again, our leaders were aware of how that approach leads to frustration and costly rework, and they made sure to allow "space to think" so that people wouldn't feel compelled to rush through the process.

Part of the concern was about morale. I like to use the analogy of a tree here. If you chop away at that tree and remove a chunk of morale each time, sooner or later the tree's going to fall. We see it at other companies quite often.

The disciplined approach to determining causes and the "space to think" were some of the key areas we developed in our Quality Circles. We kept careful check sheets of our progress, and our leaders would pay close attention not only to our PDCA process, but to how we had conducted our meetings, allowed for diverse opinions, and built consensus.

So people involvement was always embedded in the way we designed improvements. When we presented a solution to leadership for approval, which was required when there were significant budgets involved, they didn't just look at the bottom line—they looked at when we had met, whom we had involved, and what we had covered in our meetings. All this was considered part of showing that the process owner was thinking correctly.

Now, somebody used to traditional decision making might think that it's impossible to get anything done with all these rules and this accountability for every step of thinking. Actually, the opposite is true. As we discussed earlier, this kind of discipline is practiced widely throughout the organization and becomes second nature. Just like making sure you weren't even 30 seconds late for work!

BRAINSTORMING THE BEST IDEAS

This thinking made it relatively straightforward to come up with possible countermeasures. In fact, if the inquiry process has flowed as it should, developing countermeasures is far easier and more natural. It's almost like opening the floodgates.

The planning of countermeasures typically followed three steps: first we gather as many countermeasures as possible, then categorize them by considering their differences and similarities, and finally, validate them.

Step 1: Gather Countermeasures

The purpose here is to gather as many potential countermeasures as possible that will remove the root cause from the process. It's important to have a very open mind here and put our critical voice on hold.

The main idea is to avoid any restrictive thinking and allow ideas to flow. Sometimes the piggyback method can work, where an idea is given and others build upon it, and this often leads to the best solutions. In any case, there's no such thing as a bad idea, and ideas that are "way out there" are never discouraged. We also had to encourage quiet people to speak up, as my colleagues did for me many years ago. Get to Solution always requires a safe environment where ideas can be proposed freely, without fear of ridicule.

Step 2: Sort Countermeasures by Category

Once a list of possible countermeasures has been compiled, the next step is to explore what they have in common and where they differ. To do this, we can create categories that suit the problem. Some, for example, might remove the root cause with existing staff, and another group might achieve this by bringing in outside resources.

Some might be very similar or almost identical. On the other hand, there may be outliers—ideas that don't follow the same thinking as the others. None of this is bad—what we're doing here is taking stock of the possibilities. It's a little like doing a detailed inventory of ideas.

Step 3: Validate the Countermeasures

Here, we go through each potential countermeasure and test it. We ask two questions:

- Given the thinking behind this, is this really the best countermeasure we can create to eliminate the root cause?
- What actions would I (or we) need to take to implement this?

Asking these questions tends to help separate the stronger from the weaker possibilities.

NARROWING THE POSSIBILITIES

Once we have a good solid list of potential countermeasures, we adopt a more critical mode of thinking where we ask a series of tough questions. Here, rather than widening our inquiry, we are looking for potential downsides.

Here is a list of questions that we use in our sessions:

- How feasible is this countermeasure?
- Who could it impact? Next process, other departments, plants, people?
- What is the cost involved?
- What is the effectiveness of the countermeasure?
- Does it contribute to the key performance indicators of the company?
- Is there a skill set needed to implement?
- Do we have all the resources needed to implement this countermeasure?

The overriding issue here, once again, is about people, and how the proposed change would affect them. First, there is the immediate impact on the people in the process. Will they have to be trained to follow the new standard? Will it involve some initial stress as they get used to the new process?

Then there might be impact on people outside the process. It could, for example, change the way we serve our external customer, requiring people to make adjustments. Or it might require some additional training or process change from one of our upstream suppliers.

It's also important to take a hard look at potential compliance issues. When we implement a solution, the change might pose an unacceptable safety risk—an immediate showstopper. On the other hand, it could endanger compliance with government regulations, or impact a standard that the customer is used to. A large change could even have a negative impact on the surrounding community—for example, by increasing noise levels.

To keep track of the pros and cons of each solution, we assess each possibility according to several simple criteria, such as:

- Cost
- Feasibility
- Effectiveness
- Impact
- Risk

Rating systems vary. Many companies use a simple three-point rating system, while some prefer a 10-point system. Whatever your rating method is, remember that ratings are educated opinions, and they are only as valid as the thinking behind them.

Sometimes in Quality Circles, we would get a show of hands to see how many people would support each potential idea. Then, we would go back to the more popular ones, and ask the dissenters if they would be willing to support that idea since the group had a pretty good consensus on it. We would also ask what part of the countermeasure they were uncomfortable with, and if they would be willing to support it if there were changes.

Sometimes there was one outlier who was really entrenched. Here, the circle leader would say "Let's Go to See together. I want to see it through your eyes." And you would go out to the process, and then that's when you might find that the person had some personal issues. On the other hand, the person may have been aware of something that the group had overlooked.

We didn't like to leave anybody behind. This would make people in traditionally run companies impatient, but at Toyota we never lost sight of the importance of people development and maintaining the culture.

Once again, our training was crucial here. We were taught to facilitate meetings where people were upset. We learned how to handle a situation where somebody's pet idea was being rejected, and we needed that person's buy-in to continue. We learned how to listen for signs that somebody was upset. These people skills are essential to managing in any environment, especially one where respect for people is the law of the land.

Another important step we followed was to keep several ideas active as potential "Plan B's" in case the chosen solution was not successful or proved to be unfeasible after further investigation. Alternatively, we might have needed an interim solution to alleviate the symptom temporarily if a permanent solution was not feasible within a reasonable time frame.

It's important to not postpone this "Plan B" step until the need arises—it is always easiest to "strike while the iron is hot" and create the plan(s) while all the planning criteria are on the flipcharts and everybody's thinking around countermeasures is fresh.

BUY-IN ON STEROIDS

Once we've identified the best countermeasure, we're in a position to approach all affected stakeholders and say, "This is what we are planning to do, this is where we will do it, here's why, and here's how we're going to do it." However, we always followed that up with "What do you think?"

Getting buy-in isn't just about asking people to say yes—the more appropriate question might be, "Are my countermeasures correct in your view, and can you think of any ways we could improve this plan?" Stakeholders might be able to offer additional insights on areas such as:

- Technology implications, such as how a change will affect IT, or how IT could help
- Scheduling issues that you were not aware of
- New developments that weren't known when the problem was originally investigated
- Instances where a similar plan was tried before
- Team and personnel issues
- Conflicts with other improvement initiatives

Inclusiveness is critical here—it's essential that stakeholders will feel they have been heard before the changes are put into any kind of formal plan. Furthermore, there is nothing more frustrating for a team than failing to consult with all stakeholders and then missing a "hidden" showstopper that halts the entire project.

In a nutshell, consensus building is about making each countermeasure as good as it can possibly be by engaging the brain of every stakeholder. When done right, this is a triumph of what people can accomplish by thinking together.

RELIABLE MOVES CLOSER TO A SOLUTION

After identifying the root cause for the lack of support for QC projects in assembly, Clayton and Ashley consulted with Bob the Lean coordinator, and they selected a representative team of volunteers in the assembly area to develop a plan to give more support to the QC leader role.

Participants were encouraged to share as many ideas as possible, even if they seemed to be highly unconventional. They considered hiring a dedicated person for the QC role in the department. They considered having HR provide the resources for the QC role. They considered assigning the QC leader duties to team leaders and the group leader on a rotating basis. And to Clayton's surprise, a team member suggested a novel idea— that the workload in the department be rebalanced in order to make the QC coordinator into a full-time role.

Then the team evaluated each option by effectiveness, cost, and risk. Based on the evaluation, the group decided to proceed with the rebalancing option.

The plan was far more ambitious than Clayton could have imagined, yet it was coming from the people at the *gemba*. By rebalancing the workload to free up time for more improvements, they were getting the best solution possible at a minimal cost. Furthermore, this was a challenge for the people in the workplace, showed great respect for their abilities, and, Clayton noted, was right in line with his objective of developing people.

"Now we have a clear direction that everybody agrees on," said Clayton excitedly. "Next week we will get together and create a project plan that we can implement as a team."

A COMMON LANGUAGE

Alan Kandel, Global Head of Methods and Tools, Multinational Chemical Company

One of the big strengths of the A3 process is that it gives people a common language for problem solving. If I'm an engineer working on a certain problem, and I'm talking to somebody in supply chain, it may be difficult, in some cases, to come to a common understanding of a problem definition, details related to the problem, and what parts of the problem are going to be tackled first, second, etc. But when you're talking about breaking down the problem, or setting a target, or knowing that you're not going to jump into root cause analysis immediately, then everyone is focused and understands the task at hand. The team can move to a solution much faster because everybody in the room is on the same page.

CREATING AN IMPLEMENTATION PLAN

At this point, we will have come a long way. Of course, creating a project plan is usually the first step in a traditional company, where people don't even Go to See.

At Toyota, once we had gotten to this point, we'd done a thorough job of investigating based on the facts, had analyzed them using a scientific process, and had consulted in a meaningful way with all stakeholders.

When we work this way, the implementation plans we put in place don't have to be very long or complicated because we're not introducing anything that hasn't been discussed or vetted at the *gemba*. The plan is a confirmation that we are going to go ahead with a list of specifics. And it also assigns responsibilities for various roles in the plan, as well as timelines.

As an overall guideline, it's important to make sure that the plan addresses the four *W*'s:

- **Who** will be responsible for completing each particular step or action?
- **What** exactly will be the roles and responsibilities of that person? What training or development will that person require? What risks or difficulties have to be kept in

mind with this step, and what can be done to alleviate them?

- **Where** will the action take place? Are there coordination issues with other areas?
- **When** will this step begin, and when will it be complete? Here we have to show some flexibility, as constraints around scheduling can vary.

It's also important to specify in each case **how** the work will be done and **how** much that is going to cost, be that through resource use or financial cost.

The assignment of roles had various dynamics depending on the situation. One of the criteria for assignment was how experienced that person was with problem solving. When I was group leader, I would often caution team leaders, who were typically the QC leaders, not to overwhelm a person with responsibilities.

On the other hand, we wanted to have people working closest to their own process. So if somebody is going to be working to a different standard, the results are best measured by that person.

Sometimes, special skills came into play. Some people were given responsibilities because they had great artistic abilities and could really make things look nice on a flipchart, or create a nice display on a visual board. If somebody had the skills for that, we would ask the group, "Is everybody okay with this person doing the drawing or illustrations?"

Finally, there was the priority of developing the people involved, and sometimes our leaders would give us a little push outside of our comfort zone. This is where David Meier, my leader, said, "Okay, we're going to do a presentation in front of the managers. They want to see our circle process. So Tracey, will you do five minutes of the presentation?"

And that's how he got me in front of the microphone for the very first time.

THE IMPLEMENTATION TEAM TAKES OVER

When the team at Reliable met the following week, there was excitement in the air. The participants understood that this wasn't just about their area—they were experimenting with a bold new way to further the company's purpose.

The team was very methodical. They needed to determine the best person for each role based on people's capabilities and the least effort to rebalance their work. They knew that they had to map out all the work that was being rebalanced and, at the same time, determine the exact duties and responsibilities of the QC coordinator role. Finally, process owners had to be assigned for all of the steps.

The plan shown in Figure 7.3 was placed on the Wall. "Now it's up to our people to carry out the plan," said Brody-san. "They now own the process, and we must trust them to do their work. All we can do now is wait."

FINALLY—THE "DO" PHASE BEGINS

Once we got to the "Do" stage where we began to make physical changes in the work environment, the intensity increased, and the pace quickened. Here, we are changing people's work, and we have to act quickly and decisively to minimize disruption and uncover any difficulties as quickly as possible. Once we get to this stage, the emphasis is on moving quickly and deliberately, while at the same time being prepared for obstacles. To symbolize this, Toyota, in its manuals, developed a graphic of a rocket going through a wall. Our trainers recognized that we would likely be pushing through some resistance, and encouraged us here to "never give up."

Therefore, even though most of the work has been done, the implementation is perhaps the most intense, because we are now actually changing people's jobs. For example, roles might

WHAT TO IMPLEMENT	WHO	WHERE	WHEN Oct	Nov	Dec	Jan	Feb
1. Create trial process maps with each candidate in the QC role, showing balancing potential.	Specialists	Within each department	Assess-Plan				
2. Based on mapping results, investigate all the responsibilities needed to fulfill the QC Coordinator Role.				Assess-Plan			
3. If applicable, explore the need for more than one QC Coordinator, or sharing the duties with several Team Members.	Coordinator		Define – Propose – Agree – Communicate – Implement				
4. After the QC responsibilities have been delegated, develop a detailed communication plan.						Communicate to all stakeholders	
5. Solicit feedback on the QC Wall to continue improving QC activity in each department.						Monitor – Feedback – Adjust	

FIGURE 7.3 Implementing the plan

be reassigned, people might have to be cross-trained in new skill sets, or a process might be operating with fewer people. The changes might affect internal customers, or even external customers. And yes . . . there might be unanticipated delays, consequences, or problems.

And finally, people might be drawn out of their comfort zone. As we mentioned, this is generally considered positive at Toyota, that is, assuming that there is adequate communication.

The reporting and communication scheme was very thorough at TMMK, and there was standard work in how we gathered our data, checked our progress on each step, and reported to stakeholders.

There's an amusing story behind this. Once I heard a trainer talking to David Meier through an interpreter, and the interpreter asked David, "Did you eat your spinach today?" Well, I heard him ask it again the next day and thought that was kind of odd. So I asked David, "What's this about spinach? Why does he keep asking you?"

David laughed and said, "The Japanese word for spinach is *horenso*. *HoRenSo* is also the short-form term we use for *Hokoku*, *Renraku*, *Sodan*, which means Report, Update/Inform, Consult. So he's asking me if I'm keeping everybody in the loop on a project that I'm working on."

I like the analogy, because communication, like spinach, makes you stronger. However, we use a different analogy, and that's 360 degree communication (Figure 7.4). This kind of reporting was one more thing that was drummed into us at TMMK early on, and was one of the pillars of accountability. In our Quality Circles, we reported on a regular basis how our process was going, and this is how the circle leader maintained accountability for the project.

There are some practical implications here. When a project is touching new ground for people, it's important to share negative news quickly, as this could influence people's perception of the project, and might also require extra time. Negative news might

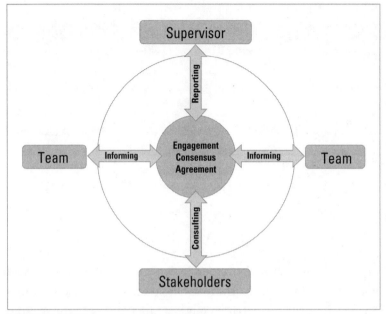

FIGURE 7.4 360 degree communication

also be a signal that extra time is required to resolve unforeseen complications, or that contingency plans need to be developed.

However, the biggest concern was always people, and showing utmost respect for any implications that the change could have for them. And remember—development of people was always seen as a major priority, regardless of the scope of the project.

In our workshops, we use the progress chart in Figure 7.5 to ensure that complete and timely communication takes place at all stages.

COPING WITH FAILURE

There's an old saying that if you fail to plan, you plan to fail. We had a slightly different take on this. Toyota, more than any company I know, used comprehensive planning to reduce the

IMPLEMENTATION STEP	REPORTING (SUPERVISOR)	INFORMING (TEAM)	CONSULTING (STAKEHOLDERS)	EVALUATION
Step 1	●	●	●	●
Step 2	●	▲	✖	▲
Step 3	●	●	▲	▲
Step 4	▲	▲	✖	▲
Step 5	▲	▲	▲	▲

● = communicated   ▲ = partial communication   ✖ = no communication

FIGURE 7.5 Communication progress chart

probability of failure. However, it also knew that no matter how much planning you do, there are no guarantees, and we must always maintain a realistic view, and be ready for failure. So if we failed, we had a plan for that, too.

Failure at Toyota is not a sign that it's time to quit. We've already established a problem and a root cause, and it is essential that this root cause be eliminated. As a result, our trainers always emphasized that we must never give up.

When a countermeasure isn't delivering the anticipated results, the first action is to ask why, and trace the precise reason for that failure. Perhaps there were unanticipated circumstances that have to be factored into the plan. Perhaps there was a flaw that nobody saw. Perhaps the change is making unreasonable demands on people. This could dictate the need for more time, revising the plan, or adopting a temporary countermeasure. In the latter case, it's always a given that until the root cause has been addressed, the problem-solving process is not complete.

Whatever the outcome, going backward and redoing a step in the A3 is not stigmatized. Continuous improvement is about trial and error, so this kind of iteration should be considered normal. And in an environment where we were always learning, we were always moving forward.

8

Get to Standardization

■ ■ ■

As we have discussed throughout this book, standards
were everywhere at TMMK, and "living" the standards
was interwoven into our daily thinking. This assimilation was based on enormous trust on the part of employees that
standards were there for a good reason—to help people meet
their expectations as members of a team that continuously
improved work to benefit the customer and the company. We
never saw standards as a hindrance because we understood the
"why," and our constant awareness of the thinking behind the
standards assisted us greatly in seeing abnormality at a glance.

When we improved a standard, we had to be cognizant
that we were making alterations to what had become a natural
way of thinking for other people. The danger is that when you
ask people to behave differently without engaging or involving
them, the change can cause resistance on a very personal level.

People in our culture were, on the other hand, very conditioned to change, and understood that standards were always
in a state of evolution. The thinking was that the "best known
method" can always get better. In fact, once a process had
become stabilized and things got comfortable, workers had

come to expect that change was in the air. Oftentimes our trainers would see it as a *problem* if a standard remained stagnant for too long—they would say, "It's too easy!"

Standards, therefore, were in various stages of evolution. This meant that people had to be aware not only of the standards in their area, but of the state of each standard in the evolutionary improvement cycle. To help people maintain that awareness, we've developed an acronym, DAMI, which stands for:

- **Define** the standard: Define the expected results based on internal and external customer needs.
- **Achieve** the standard: Establish predictability and repeatability.
- **Maintain** the standard: Maintain and audit the standard to achieve expected results.
- **Improve** the standard: Raise the bar on the standard to purposely create a gap.

In our workshops, we recommend that people use DAMI to maintain a mental picture of the current state of each standard. We have found that this is a powerful way to visualize the progress of continuous improvement in the organization.

CHANGE WITH DISCIPLINE

In Toyota's improvement culture, anybody who takes action to improve a standard must be able to demonstrate the "why" based on hard measures. Instead of saying, "We did a project, and we need you to change your standard work," we must be able to say, "Engaging with the people doing the work, we've found a way to alleviate a problem that was compromising our ability to satisfy our customers, and we've proven that by adopting the new standard, we will move the needle."

Essentially, anybody introducing a new standard must have confirmed through process measures that the proposed change really will close the intended gap. This involves arriving at a consensus based on looking very carefully at the results, and tying them all the way back to the gap that we had identified earlier on.

Therefore, in step 7 of the eight steps, we practiced a special kind of due diligence before declaring that a new countermeasure would become standard work. We began with the most fundamental question: Did the countermeasure achieve our target? The emphasis here was to be objective and not try to "spin" our results by saying something like "Yes, sort of." We need to answer definitively whether the countermeasure met the ultimate goal for the company as defined by the KPI contribution, whether it met internal and external customer needs, and very important, what we learned through the process.

The fact is, if a countermeasure does not deliver to expectations, this is not a failure—it just means that there is more work to be done to remove the root cause. And since we've already established that the root cause is standing in the way of our objectives, it remains urgent that we take it on with the same determination that we applied when we began the project.

There were different levels of intervention here. Sometimes we would return to the process to ensure that something wasn't overlooked in the implementation. Sometimes we would bring in a short-term or temporary countermeasure that would give us the time to recreate the problem for a more long-term countermeasure. It all depended on the circumstances. However, regardless of the situation, nothing could actually be called a solution until the experimentation and trials of the countermeasure were complete and it was proven that the countermeasure or countermeasures completely addressed the root cause.

Our inquiry, however, was not limited to looking at results. We also looked at the project itself, and how well the planning and implementation worked. Was there a better way we could

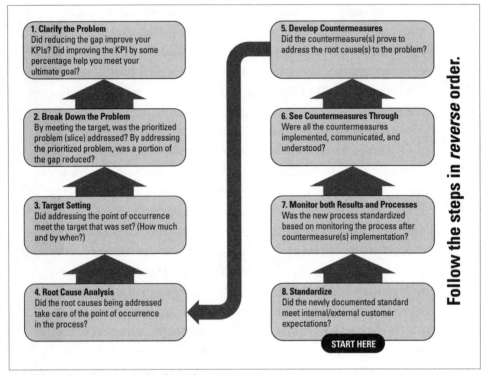

FIGURE 8.1 Reading the A3 backward

have done this? Did the people involved feel comfortable with the process, and did they develop new capabilities?

To help get the big picture here, we teach a method in our sessions that we call "reading the A3 backward." Essentially, we look in sequence at the earlier steps to confirm that the linkages have taken place (Figure 8.1).

For example, as we implemented our countermeasures in Step 6, was the root cause that we developed in Step 4 truly validated, or did we discover indications that we could be on the wrong track? Was the point of occurrence that we identified truly accurate, or were there other irregularities contributing to the problem? Were we truly closing the gap that we had committed to closing when we began the project, and furthermore, could we prove that this was the result of removing the root cause?

These questions are particularly pertinent because sometimes we get lucky and get great results from a project that was poorly planned or executed. In traditional companies, of course, managers immediately claim credit for their brilliance whenever they get a lucky break. At TMMK, we were very aware of that tendency and made sure that we could prove our results were not just due to a happy roll of the dice.

Once we had thoroughly analyzed our results and processes, we shared our thinking with our stakeholders. Note that before actually creating a new standard, we are once again validating our thinking, this time with the people that we're going to depend on for the new standard to be successful.

A NEW TAKE ON THE A3

Tanya Doyle, Lean Culture Coach

A3 gets thrown around a lot as some kind of tool, but really, A3 is just a European size of paper that we use to record our thinking. Tracey really drives home that it's not just writing down a bunch of steps, it's being able to answer questions like, "Why am I even talking about this?" and "What exactly am I trying to solve?"

In my first class with Tracey, I was sort of going through the motions with an A3 exercise and working my way through the steps. I thought I was doing pretty well—I had my goal, and then I had the current condition. I think was already halfway through the right side of the page when she was tapping me on my shoulder.

"Hey, if we take this backward, and we go from the right side to the left side, are your countermeasures really going to fix that gap?"

It was a little like using subtraction or addition to check your math just like we did when we were little. Here, we've done all this work, and now we're checking to make sure it flows all the way back up, and it's going to take care of the problem. This was a huge "aha" moment for me.

LOOKING AT THE FUTURE STATE

After we had completed the evaluation of the project itself, we entered another stage of due diligence—an inquiry into how the new standard would fit into the work environment. What would it be like to have this countermeasure as the new standard? We approached this from several different angles:

- Will our *customers* benefit from this change, and if so, how?
- Will this change help us move forward toward our *company* goals?
- Will the new standard be good for our *people* in terms of their daily work and their long-term development?

These questions, of course, are not new—we would have explored them throughout the process of investigating and developing the change. What's new here is the context. Now we have a defined change that's been proven to work, and that equips us with the facts we need to conduct a productive inquiry into the overall impact of that change.

In considering these questions, we would always pause for reflection. If there was a concern that there might be some repercussions from the change, such as a longer than expected learning curve, we always asked why, and sought to have a deeper understanding. There is no such thing as a plan that goes perfectly, so we always sought to learn the hidden lessons that the project had taught us.

As well, our reflections didn't always yield a definite yes or no. In some such cases, we would set up a trial run of the new standard before implementing the new change. For example, if the new standard involved using a new container, we might run the process with a temporary cardboard version of the container as a test before we asked Tool and Die to make us a permanent one. In some cases, this would uncover potential gaps that we hadn't accounted for.

Once we had thoroughly evaluated our results, considered the possible implications of the new standard, reflected on all the lessons learned, and verified that all expectations could be met, it was time to create the new standard.

ENCOURAGING SIGNS AT RELIABLE

Six months after initiating the project on QC participation, the rebalancing was complete, and the Assembly department was starting to show some impressive results around Quality Circle activity. Nine new projects had gotten off the ground, and it looked like with a full-time QC coordinator, Assembly was in line to become the top QC contributor in the company.

"I think we're making some real progress on our culture problem," said Clayton excitedly to Brody-san. But the wise sensei knew that in a continuous improvement environment, the due diligence never ends.

"What if this was just luck?" he asked.

Clayton was stunned to hear this from Brody-san after all the hard work, and there was an awkward silence. However, as he reflected on this, he had to admit that even with these great results, he couldn't actually prove that they were directly tied to the countermeasures they had implemented. He had completed all the steps correctly in the A3 and had applied all the correct thinking—what more could he do?

"How can I know for sure that this wasn't just luck?" he asked.

"The answer is in your A3," said Brody-san. Clayton stared at his A3, puzzled.

"Read your A3 backward," said Brody-san. "Go through the steps backward and see if everything you have done has actually turned out as you had predicted, and has in fact closed the gap."

Reading the A3 backward was an illuminating experience. It reminded Clayton of his accounting courses, where you double-check your numbers. Looking backward, we could see a chain of events. The countermeasure attacked the root cause and met the target at the point of occurrence. All of this traced back to the original gap that had been defined months earlier.

Clayton shared his reasoning with Brody-san. Now they had a better system for supporting their Quality Circle program. Any department could benefit from this approach, and if it became the new standard, it would accelerate the continuous improvement activity and the development of people throughout the company.

"Good," said Brody-san. "Now we are ready to share the wisdom with other departments."

So a presentation was arranged. Kim, who was very shy, was selected as the presenter. She was not the most experienced presenter, but selecting Kim was another opportunity to develop an employee.

MORE THAN A PIECE OF PAPER

Kelly Moore, Operational Excellence Lead, Syngenta LLC

A3 has become a fad these days, and for a lot of people, this is about following the steps and creating a paper document. So, one of the things I tell people is that there's A3 the piece of paper, and then there's A3 the methodology, and we're concentrating on the methodology. We'll end up with a piece of paper, but we don't really care about that. What we really want to focus on is how we got there.

The same applies in a way to standard work. I tell people we have standard work the noun, the piece of paper, and then there's the verb, which is all the behavior and thinking behind that. We have to be clear which one we're talking about because they might mean different things to different people.

CREATING THE NEW STANDARD

A new standard is, in a very basic sense, a tool for replicating a successful countermeasure for anybody facing similar circumstances. What's required, therefore, is more than an abbreviated "reminder" for people who were involved in a project—the new standard must function as a practical guide for somebody with no prior knowledge of the project.

For a simple process, the standard might be a single sheet that lists the major steps or specifications for the new way of doing a job. If the process is more complex, it might be necessary to create a more formal document such as a manual, a work instruction, or a set of Job Breakdown sheets. Training would also have to be designed, arranged, and provided in such cases.

Regardless of the scope and complexity, it's important to create the standard with the end user in mind. If a person you had never met, working in some remote part of the business, were to adopt this standard, what would it be like for him or her? How could we be sure that that person is able to adjust to this new way of working without undue stress? Respect for this unseen person is just as important as respect for your neighboring coworkers.

A great example of this kind of thinking can be found in retail operations such as Lowe's, whose success depends on customers being able to comfortably navigate their very large store environments. The idea is to have consistent standards for floor layouts, shelf arrangements, and visual displays that allow first-time customers to quickly get a sense of where they can find what they need. These companies do a significant amount of research and testing to get this right, and if you look carefully at how these stores are set up, you'll be able to see just how effective this standardization is.

With this thinking in mind, we need to consider any additional information that will help the users of the standard be successful. If you've just come out of a successful *kaizen*, you will often be aware of a large amount of peripheral information that pertains only indirectly to the work. For example, you may know that a project similar to yours wasn't successful because a particular circumstance wasn't known. Sharing this with potential users may help remove hesitancy on their part, or help them stay on guard for possible complications.

On the other hand, there's sometimes a tendency to share too much information. Especially in the technical world, people get pretty excited about the subtleties of the reasoning behind what they did and the knowledge that they applied and gained. Remember that users like to see a clear, step-by-step guide that's easy to follow and internalize. People have hundreds of standards to follow as it is, so you need to show respect for their time and attention, regardless of their level in the organization.

SHARING THE STANDARD WITH OTHERS

Once a standard is distributed and gets used by others, we enter the next realm of testing and accountability. The fact that a countermeasure was proven to be successful for the group that tested it doesn't prove that the new standard representing that countermeasure will be successful with other groups. The standard may not be clear, may fail to address a variety of possible circumstances, or may have missed process defects that didn't surface during the testing of the countermeasure.

Consequently, standards, just like the processes they document, are subject to scientific testing and continuous improvement. As introduced in Chapter 2, we created, maintained, and improved the quality of our standards using SDCA, the acronym for Standardize, Do, Check, Act.

In many cases, particularly if an A3 was involved, we would have tested the previous standard using SDCA, leading to the conclusion that we needed to change the process itself in order to close a gap. The logic here is that you ensure you're following the current standard before you react and change the process. Once we've gone ahead and changed the process, we return to SDCA to ensure that the new standard will deliver successful results for all stakeholders.

The process unfolds as follows:

- **Standardize.** Begin asking questions at the process, specifying the needs based on the internal and external customer's expectations, taking into account all practical issues, and involving all stakeholders. Incorporate experiments/trials to test the repeatability and achievability of the new standard. Gain consensus and buy-in on the creation of the standard.
- **Do.** Put the standard in place as the "best known method at the moment that everyone agrees to be accountable to until improvements are made and agreed upon." Develop a training program based on a standardized method such as job instruction training (JIT) or training within the industry (TWI) steps. Develop a mechanism for accountability with measures to ensure that the standard meets the customer expectation. Post the standard so that it become accessible to all stakeholders through visual displays at the process, or in a designated reference area.

- **Check.** Continue to audit and measure to verify that effectiveness is being maintained. Make any necessary adjustments or modifications if needed. Track for a period of time to create stability. Guard against the tendency to implement rapid changes without documentation, as this creates chaos and harms continuous improvement.
- **Act.** Once the standard meets the above expectations and is delivering desired results in a predictable fashion, reinforce the standard and ensure that it is being followed. The new standard now becomes the new benchmark for future improvements.

In a nutshell, SDCA complements our PDCA efforts by ensuring that the standard truly represents the improvements that we've tested and provides all of the information and guidelines that users and stakeholders require in order to implement the improvement successfully. Over time, the standard stabilizes, and it gets assimilated into the daily work flow.

This is the point where people may think that they can wipe their brow and rest. In our culture at Toyota, however, we knew that we were entering one of the most important phases of continuous improvement.

9

Get to Sustainability

■ ■ ■

Sustaining sounds like it should be easy. You've made measurable progress, and you've proven that it wasn't just luck. You've documented all the steps that got you there, and created a new standard for everybody to follow. Now all you have to do is stick to the path you have created. The hard work is already done, so there's no problem here, right?

Wrong!

Sustain is perhaps the most misunderstood aspect of continuous improvement. Not only is the work to sustain just as hard as the work that created the gains in the first place, but the difficulties here tend to catch people off guard, leaving them confused and discouraged. "We were doing so well—what happened?" is something we hear in a lot of companies.

To illustrate what we're up against, I'd like to use a sports analogy. As we were finishing up the manuscript of this book, the Chicago Cubs won their first World Series in 108 years, ending the longest drought in baseball history. Essentially, they'd been working to this goal for 108 years. Along the way, they had ups and downs, with some better years and then some years that were terrible, but they were learning as they pursued the ultimate goal of winning that World Series title.

Now let's consider a hypothetical question. If the Cubs do everything they did this year, will they win the World Series next year? I can guarantee you that the answer is no. They will have to continue to make changes if they are to be successful. In fact, without the aspirational goal of ending that 108-year drought, it's going to be even more difficult. And when that reality hits, you are sure to see a lot of discouraged Cubs fans.

We see the same pattern with companies that adopt Lean. In the early days, they are discovering the tools and their potential, and there's great excitement and rapid progress. Then, once the novelty of this new approach has worn off, the organization faces the hard work of "normalizing" Lean thinking so that it is followed day in and day out. What was a blitz event turns into a journey with no end—and no end to the hard work.

Here's where the energy level begins to drop—a little like coming off a sugar high—and people begin to give up. For most companies, this is the turning point that decides if Lean will be a true transformation or another "flavor of the month."

WE CAN NEVER RELAX

Jon Miller, Co-Founder, Gemba Academy

Becoming satisfied with the way things are is the first step backward, but most people don't realize this. When things are good and working well, we relax. Then we start backsliding. The constant eye for things that can be improved, developing others to see their work environment that way, and making this a culture is a huge part of what has helped Toyota succeed.

SUSTAINING AT TMMK

In 1990, TMMK won the coveted J. D. Power Gold Plant Quality Award. For a plant that had been in production for less than two years, this was a phenomenal achievement. Especially when you consider that most team members, Ernie and I included, had no prior experience in the automotive industry.

However, we had won, and now had to face the question of sustaining that level of performance. In this situation, you might expect a conservative strategy that locked in the gains by keeping everything as stable as possible.

TMMK, however, took a very different path. Our sales were growing so rapidly in the early nineties that we needed to dramatically increase our capacity. To accommodate this, our leaders decided to build a second plant that modeled our existing one. Furthermore, they decided that TMMK employees would be involved in building that plant.

So here we were, right in the middle of learning how we could sustain the first plant that was still so new, and at the same time doubling our size by starting up a second plant. And so we had to sustain that label of being a J.D. Power Gold Plant amongst a rapid pace of promotions, training, development, construction, and movement of personnel—all of which created a baseline of instability.

At the time, I honestly felt we were being pushed over the limit. But our leaders were able to say, "This is going to push us, and it's going to take us to new limits, but we have the stability in our business model that allows to make those changes and move forward. We will move forward because that's the way we do business." Ultimately, Mr. Cho, our president, had a vision that we could build that second plant, even though many would have argued that we were not ready for it.

So, amongst all this upheaval, could we win the Gold Plant award again? It turned out that we had some tough competition from Toyota Motor Manufacturing Canada (TMMC) the following year and had to settle for Silver, and then for Bronze in '92. But we remained on the podium, and we were back on top to capture Gold in '93 and '94.

The reality is that we had to do a lot more than sustain—competing against other Toyota plants, we had no choice but to get better!

THE TRUE MEANING OF SUSTAIN

Sustaining, to be honest, is a bit of an illusion. People think that consistent behavior ensures consistent results, but that's sadly not the case. In our dynamic world, dozens of factors threaten our stability. Customer specifications change, causing processes to have to be redesigned and creating unanticipated instability for neighboring processes. Supplier capabilities evolve, creating either constraints or new options. And of course, market conditions are always in flux, forcing organizations to find ways to deliver faster, cheaper, and better. As pointed out earlier, a 1988 Toyota Camry wouldn't meet today's expectations of our automotive market.

Internal factors can be equally daunting. When organizations lose key people, they often struggle to maintain processes that have become dependent on expertise or on leadership capabilities. As we saw, the rapid promotion of people at TMMK in the early nineties created enormous challenges for maintaining stability.

Get to Sustainability involves staying one step ahead of all of these possibilities and anticipating any threats to hard-won gains. Let's look at how we do that.

FOLLOWING AND IMPROVING

Jon Miller, Co-Founder, Gemba Academy

"Please do things the way I say. Now, please change it." Following standards and changing them seems contradictory, but this feeling goes away when we recognize that in a culture that embraces continuous improvement, standards are not there mainly to maintain but as a basis for improvement. A standard is not the platform on which you stand, but a step on the ladder before the next one you take. At a minimum, standards must change because various conditions in real life change, such as what customers expect, the people who do the work, the materials and information inputs, or the equipment and technology that we use to do our work. If we become satisfied or complacent and don't change the standards while these factors change, we are in fact getting worse. Even when these factors remain exactly the same, we can always find better methods.

A WINDOW ON THE FUTURE

As most people are aware, executives often manage their progress with the help of key performance indicators (KPIs). These fall into two categories: *lagging indicators* and *leading indicators*. Lagging indicators are results-oriented, in that they appear *after* the fact. Some would say they're historical in nature, since they are often a reaction to what has already taken place, perhaps months ago. In the car industry, this could be the number of warranty claims filed with dealerships for creaky suspensions.

Leading indicators, on the other hand, are KPIs that are tracking right at the process. This gives us a real-time measure as to when we may be out of standard or don't have what is needed when it's needed to produce our service or output.

The beauty of leading indicators is that they provide an immediate picture of how well the organization is doing, as opposed to a report based on lagging indicators that could be delayed for weeks or months.

Consider safety, for example—let's suppose that a team member in an automotive plant gets injured during a work process. This gets documented on an incident-rate report in most organizations. This means that we're tracking an injury after it already happened.

This is a necessary process in most organizations due to OSHA or other safety mandates, but the question we have to ask is, "What does this information tell us about the process in which the incident occurred?" If the actual incident happened one to three days before the report came out, are we able to know what really caused it? Maybe, but reconstructing incidents is not easy, and tends to be very unreliable. Listening to how different witnesses recall the details of an accident in a courtroom reveals how difficult this is.

That incident-rate report typifies the way KPIs are tracked in most industries—not just manufacturing. The problem here is that incident-rate reports tend to overlook the very trends that cause injuries. Managers, however, tend to mistakenly believe that they have sufficient information from these lagging indicators to prevent injuries and other problems.

Leading indicators, on the other hand, give us that predictive capability so that we can act before the injury actually happens. If someone mentioned "this flow rack is very high, and I have to reach several times a day," that might be a leading indicator that an accident is waiting to happen. Maybe there was a near-miss incident that hinted at a larger problem. When monitored and tracked, this kind of information can contribute to real progress in reducing accidents.

Now safety is only one example of leading and lagging indicators. A creaky suspension could have been caused by changing a component without doing a proper quality assessment, which in turn might have been due to a quality assessment process not being kept up to date. And a late delivery might be traced back to machine downtime, which could be traced to a poorly designed maintenance plan. The point is, all roads lead to process here, and that's where we have to focus to stay ahead of problems.

So, how do you start identifying your leading indicators? Essentially, you need to take a closer look at your daily processes. Asking questions of your team members about how their process is going, and whether or not there are issues, can help you Grasp the Situation of predictive measure versus reactive.

An effective strategy is to establish a regular "how's your process" (HYP) check. This creates a daily touchpoint so the supervisor can go to see if there are any emerging issues. In the safety example, this is then logged on a visual management chart for safety and posted daily. If something goes wrong it gives us a very specific window of time to track the discrepancy. Even a simple check like this can greatly reduce incident rates, and can help the organization evolve toward a more proactive stance.

The point is, every process in the organization is subject to deterioration if leading indicators aren't monitored and heeded. We live in a dynamic world where conditions, external and internal, are constantly changing, so there can be no such thing as a permanent standard.

So Get to Sustainability is really a journey that never ends. Whenever there is success based on a new countermeasure, we know that this will not survive unless we work constantly to preserve the gains that we have made. TMMK was very conscious of this, and kept us worrying that what works today may not meet expectations tomorrow.

EXTENDING THE LIFE OF A MINE

Frank Wagener, Continuous Improvement Manager, Mining Sector

When you're mining gold like we are, there tends to be an end of life not too far in the future where it is no longer economical to operate the mine. I've been in mining for 30 years, and I've seen all kinds of situations. I was at a mine that closed suddenly and 600 people got laid off in one day.

However, by making a mine more efficient, you make it economical to go after deposits that are harder to get at, and that in turn extends people's jobs. So there's a real incentive for everybody to get on board to help do that—you could say that we have this built-in True North.

Tracey and Ernie are helping us engage everybody in improvement projects, which can have a real impact. One of our success stories involved a satellite mine, which is five miles away from our main site. The work on these sites involves leaching gold out of clay, and the clay is very different at this site. Initially that site was operating way below expectations, and it looked like we might not even recoup the $40 million it cost to get the site up and running.

Applying what we learned in the workshops, we brought a team together from different departments and got them working toward a common objective. This allowed us to analyze the entire process at this site and come up with a unique blending strategy that had not been used before at our site. Today, the site is producing more gold than expected, extending its life and the jobs of everybody working there.

The amazing thing is that this came from people in the field who asked, "How can we do this better?" and then found answers and took the necessary initiatives to extend the life of the mine. This really empowers people to say, "Wow, I can make a difference." And as you can imagine, these projects really affect morale.

THE MOST IMPORTANT LEADING INDICATOR OF ALL

As we've emphasized throughout the book, the primary concern for leaders was always developing people. Consequently, sustaining Toyota's work culture was considered an expectation of our job, and any leading indicators that signaled a threat to the culture were quickly addressed.

Senior managers, therefore, reacted immediately to circumstances that might lead to potential morale issues. If machinery wasn't working properly, they were as worried about worker frustration as they were about slowed production. And if there were broader concerns that development of people wasn't where it should be, leaders would be sent to Japan, sometimes for months at a time, to give them a deeper understanding of the cultural thinking we were trying to create.

It was common for our leaders all the way up to the president to walk up to a team member on the line and ask, "How's your day going?" and then "How's the family?" Ernie and I both remember Mr. Cho visiting our areas several times, just asking questions and offering to help in any way possible. Our thoughts truly mattered to him and to Toyota, and that was the biggest secret of sustaining our unique culture.

SUSTAINING THE GAINS AT RELIABLE

A few months after the QC project success, Clayton was having a conversation with Brody-san. Things felt remarkably better at Reliable—people were taking more initiative to do projects, and the number of QC projects was up significantly in several departments.

"I feel we're really moving the needle on our culture," said Clayton. "I feel like we've arrived."

But Brody-san frowned. "Your people have made some great progress here," he said, "but sustaining it is going to be even more difficult than people think. It will take a lot of discipline to avoid the trap of complacency that could destroy everything you worked so hard for."

"Remember that QC program participation was maintaining before you brought me in," he continued, "and then things declined. This can happen again, but the reason will be different. And furthermore, market conditions are always changing."

"Yes," Clayton admitted, "We've read some industry reports that say the North American market is about to become a lot more competitive. That could put a lot of pressure on us."

"So you will have to get much better," said Brody-san, "or else you might discover one day that your standard is no longer good enough."

"How will we know when it isn't good enough?" asked Clayton.

"By the time you know that, it may already be too late," said Brody-san. "You must always Go to See, stay close to the *gemba*, and make sure that you are following more leading type indicators, not just lagging indicators."

Clayton immediately understood the point. Of course, every standard must always be scrutinized for improvements. The question is never "Is this good enough?" It must always be "How can we do better?"

10

Get to Stretch

■ ■ ■

In my early days as a group leader at TMMK, I was responsible for the injection molding parts-painting process—we made the interior plastic pieces for the Camry and Avalon at the time. One afternoon, one of my trainers decided to pay a visit to my area.

These *gemba* visits weren't unusual, but this time he remained for almost an hour. First, he observed the parts-painting team's standard work, glancing occasionally at the results displayed on my key performance indicator (KPI) boards. Then he began pacing back and forth, observing my entire work cell, often pausing to reflect. I could see that he was thinking very intensely.

Then suddenly, he approached me and said, "Tracey-san, we need to have a discussion about your processes and KPI boards."

I was thinking, "You know, he spent over 45 minutes out there. I went over everything he saw on my board, and I'm quite sure that everything is meeting expectation. Maybe I've finally trumped the trainer." I figured I might be even getting a well-deserved "attagirl" after all the failures I had experienced leading and learning at TMMK.

But as we walked over to my KPI board, I could tell that there was something on his mind. He was looking at me very seriously, and hesitating because, although he knew exactly what he wanted to say, he couldn't always find the right English words. Then, looking toward the injection moulding parts painting cell, he said, "Tracey-san, you have 10 people working in the parts painting team—please do this with 9 people. So *go thinking* and consider this a challenge for you." He gestured politely for me to walk away and think about what the deeper lesson was.

I was stunned. It's not that I thought this was about layoffs or forcing people to work harder—that didn't happen in our culture. But here I was, expecting praise for meeting my current expectations, and instead, I was being challenged to not only rebalance my line, but gain buy-in and consensus from my team. I figured they would likely feel as overwhelmed as I did.

However, after some reflection, I began to grasp the meaning behind my trainer's actions. The first lesson for me was that no matter how good our results look, there is still waste hidden in our processes, and we can never afford to stop looking for continuous improvement opportunities.

My trainer asked me to join him the next day at my KPI board to continue our discussion. He articulated in his best English how to differentiate between what we often see in our processes and what we are measuring, and how these differences can affect our performance according to the known standard. He asked probing questions, such as, "What are the measurements telling you? Are they a value-added measurement? Are they predictive, or are you reacting to what you input on the sheet daily or weekly?"

He also explained that a team member was needed for minor model change additions to the bumper paint line, and with the rebalance in my area, we could transition one of my people into that role. This was, therefore, an opportunity to absorb additional work by identifying waste, thereby increasing productivity with the same number of people. It was also a great development opportunity for that person, myself, and the rest of my team.

He reminded me that if your KPI indicators have been meeting expectation for too long, it *should* be a common practice to purposely raise the bar on the standard. Consequently, you have to create a gap or a problem when you don't have one, which, of course, is exactly what my trainer did. This is exactly what Taiichi Ohno was referring to when he said, "Having no problem is the biggest problem of all."

Often, raising the bar was about simply changing a target. When a documented process had stabilized to a state where internal and external customer expectations were being met consistently, then it was "fair game" to make the target more difficult.

For example, if your scrap rate was 1.5 percent and you had met that standard for a period of time, there would be an evaluation to consider 1 percent as the new standard. This raising of the bar would give you a 0.5 percent gap to problem solve. And remember, having a gap to solve was considered a good thing.

At this point, many might ask, "When is the right time to raise the bar and create a problem? Is there a magic time frame?" The short answer would be, as soon as possible once people are comfortable with the process and their results, and stability has been confirmed. When my trainer saw how comfortable I was in parts painting, he didn't waste any time!

CHANGE AS PART OF THE CULTURE

After I had spent some time looking more deeply into my processes in order to rebalance the line, the waste that my trainer had seen became very clear to me. I remember thinking, "How did I not see the waste in those 10 team members' processes?"

It took us three months to make the modifications and improvements. We started Quality Circles, and the team members got involved from both shifts. There was even some cross-functional discussion with the conveyance groups and production control. They gave their valuable input on line layout, flow rack placement, and visual controls, as well as standardized work.

Through our work, ergonomics were improved, walking was reduced, and machine wait time was eliminated. When we had successfully completed all the rebalance iterations, the entire line was reconfigured so that the work was evenly dispersed, eliminating *mura* (unevenness), *muri* (overburden), and *muda* (waste). As a result, the processes ran more fluidly with 9 people than they had with 10.

As this unfolded, it became clear that my trainer had known all along that this was possible because he had studied not only the parts-painting process, but the roles of all the stakeholders in the process and their ability to contribute to a solution. The depth of thinking and awareness that our TMMK trainers applied, passed down from the original architects of the Toyota Production System, was phenomenal, and it was a blessing to learn from them.

Of course, it would have been very easy for the trainer to just tell me what to do, but his intentions went far beyond just rebalancing head count in my area. His role was to guide and develop me to see discrepancy, and to help me create a learning environment where team members could grow their ideas and learn to see waste before the leader does.

That is a demonstration of knowledge sharing at its best. Here, the leader becomes the conduit to remove the barriers and constraints so that the ideas of his or her team members come to life. As I continued to grow in the Toyota Way, there was nothing I found more rewarding than having my Quality Circle team come in and say, "Hey, Tracey, we have some ideas to rebalance the line." In other words, they were getting ready to make improvements on their own with me as a facilitator. It is priceless when the learning process comes full circle and you have created self-directed work teams that just need you to be a servant leader.

THE IMPERATIVE TO DEVELOP PEOPLE

John Shook, Chairman and CEO, Lean Enterprise Institute

No organization, Toyota included, is "waste-free" or has the shortest possible lead time, or perfect quality each and every time. What characterizes Toyota is a relentless focus on not just solving the many problems that separate us from perfection, but at the same time developing problem-solving capability throughout the organization.

LIFE IN THE FAST LANE

Staying ahead of the market, as we did very successfully at TMMK, had a snowball effect—the more we succeeded, the faster we grew, and the quicker we had to change our processes. I remember that as we grew and doubled our size, there was a lot more AGV (automated guided vehicle) traffic in the plant, and it started to be a safety concern. To address this, standards had to be upgraded to ensure that every team member who crossed an intersection had to follow a standard "stop-point-call" process. Needless to say, this had to be incorporated into many work standards.

Our leaders, however, never put improvement on the back shelf to accommodate this rapid growth. Instead of saying "our numbers are terrific—let's just keep up with demand," they were wary of complacency and constantly looked for opportunities to make us even better as we grew. This meant that when there weren't gaps due to not meeting standards or from growth, leaders would be creating them.

To clarify, there are two kinds of gaps—*caused gaps* and *created gaps*. A *caused gap* is the kind we saw in Chapter 6 ("Grasp the Situation"), where there is a discrepancy causing a standard to not be met. The gap in that case was a stated fact, and we acted in order to close it and meet the standard.

A *created gap*, on the other hand, is about raising the standard. Here, a leader sees an opportunity for improvement and challenges people to close the gap between the way things are and the way they could be at that higher level of performance.

Created gaps, however, didn't come "out of the blue"—our leaders had long-term plans based on the company's strategic planning goals. At the same time, they were very sensitive to our environment. Often, they would be acting according to one or more circumstances.

When my trainer challenged me to rebalance my process for nine people, he had two priorities in mind. First, there was a need to move a person to bumper paint for minor model changes. In keeping with our culture, leaders were on the lookout for a way to fill this role with existing personnel—this was always our first option rather than just hiring, due to the long-term investment that Toyota makes in employees.

Secondly, the company had a personal development plan for me, and the major rebalancing that I was called upon to lead was the kind of experience I needed to improve my leadership skills at that stage.

Finally, there was enough waste in my process that this new standard was achievable. It wasn't apparent to me at first, but from his many years of experience, my trainer was able to see this, as well as how my team and I would develop through the transition.

PROBLEM SOLVING AND CREATED GAPS

Scott Powell, Director, Operational Excellence, Export Development Canada

As providers of financial products, we're expected to deliver faster and faster, and we have a strong strategy geared at making sure we remain relevant. This includes a lot of stretch metrics around creating new products and finding new platforms for existing ones, and that's forcing us to drive new standards and new processes. I would say we have become pretty activist at creating gaps.

When Tracey and Ernie talked about the distinction between created versus caused gaps, that was a big turning point for people in this company. It really helped people lock onto the idea that you might approach these differently, but you still apply the same basic A3 thinking where you slow down and think things through.

So you can see that this raising of the bar was very carefully thought out. While I was being given a huge challenge, there was lots of coaching and support throughout the transition, and the situation was carefully monitored to make sure that the change was not causing undue stress to me or to my people. The degree of planning and respect for people that my leaders displayed throughout was phenomenal.

We try to apply these lessons when we work with companies, and there are several situations that we run into on a regular basis. First of all, people think they can improve when they have no standards, so they go creating gaps that have no connection with anything measurable. We see people saying, "We want to get 50 percent better" with no idea how they will achieve that, and of course, they don't achieve anything. As

Yogi Berra said, "If you don't know where you're going, you'll wind up someplace else."

As well, organizations don't have concrete plans for developing people, which is the most important requirement for being able to raise the bar. When organizations want to move forward with continuous improvement, we often encourage them to focus their journey around people, just as Toyota does.

We worked with a company, for example, that wanted to implement Lean thinking throughout its organization. This became a three-year process around the development of people in the organization, addressing a number of knowledge and training gaps so that at the end of the process, we could wean ourselves from the project knowing that the company was no longer dependent on us.

And by the way, working ourselves out of a job is our own True North as trainers and consultants, just as it was for our trainers who had come over from Japan for a limited time. This reinforces the idea that our customers must accept the challenge of raising the bar and developing their people, and it allows us to move on and share our wisdom with the next organization.

RAISING THE BAR

Deanna Hall, Associate, Mining Sector

We actually have a motto here, and it's "Raise the bar." What that means is that you're always learning, and you're always challenged to be better. If you did great last year, next year you have to do even better. And I think that's part of the stretch, always challenge to be a little better.

DAILY COMMUNICATION
AROUND CHANGE

As mentioned earlier, we never got to "settle in" or get used to a standard very long before it changed on us (through a specific improvement process, of course). At first this was frustrating, but then as the purpose of this was explained to us, it became our norm.

In order to maintain trust and avoid firefighting situations, Toyota maintained regular communication through five-minute information sessions that were held at the end of our breaks. There were two of these every day, and they kept us in touch with changes to standards and other information pertinent to our work and gave us the opportunity to air our questions or concerns. This regular practice ensured that communication always remained a top priority.

This same communication process was used at the department level, team level, and individual process level. No matter what change was made in any area, it was always ensured that people understood the details of the change and, equally important, why it was implemented. Imposing a change "out of the blue," or rapid change without a standard in place that is so common in many companies, is considered off-limits in Toyota, as it violates the principle of respect for people.

Communication continued at our processes, and as leaders, we had the ongoing responsibility of making sure our people were properly informed and never blindsided by change. Our leaders were there as mentors from the beginning, coaching us on the proper use of the process and making sure we engaged in dialogue at the *gemba* with the people who would be affected by the change. Once this became well established, it wasn't seen as anything special—just another expectation of our job.

RELIABLE TURNS A CORNER

A year after Clayton brought Brody-san into the organization, things were looking up at Reliable. Quality Circle participation was approaching 65 percent companywide, and Quality Circles were now improving all aspects of the business, including many of the nonmanufacturing functions.

However, Clayton was disappointed when Ashley, the group leader who had played a pivotal role in the original Quality Circles project, left Reliable because she wanted to stretch herself further. The company had invested a lot in Ashley, so this was quite a loss.

Brody-san, however, was philosophical. "It's hard to lose good people," he said, "but this happens in our industry. As Zig Ziglar said, 'It's better to train people and lose them than not train people and keep them.' Now, you need to look ahead at the opportunity Ashley's departure presents for other people to develop."

"There's an important lesson here," continued Brody-san. "People always need to feel challenged, and to even be pushed a little so that they will step outside of their comfort zone. Leaders need to always be on the lookout for opportunities to provide new challenges, and they need to constantly encourage people to try new things, even if they might fail along the way."

Clayton thought about all they had accomplished, yet there was so much more to do. The opportunities for developing people were certainly not lacking. Yes, they were doing much better in their Quality Circle program, but there were still many people in the company who were not participating. Clayton didn't have to ask what the ideal state was—it was 100 percent.

"If you want to create the excitement of a challenging environment," said Brody-san, "you need to make challenge a part of everyday life for every employee."

Creating this culture of participation would require something that Brody-san called E³—Everybody Everyday Engaged. We'll talk about this in Part 3.

3

Everybody Everyday Engaged

"Senior management is simply a flag-bearer when a business decision is made. It is of no use unless others follow the flag."

—Eiji Toyoda

11

Management That Puts People First

■ ■ ■

One morning, I (Ernie) got a call from our maintenance department alerting me of an equipment problem. At the time, I had recently been promoted to production manager in TMMK's Powertrain area, which is located about a mile away from the regular plant.

It was not uncommon for us to have downtime, and we would follow the principle of *jidoka* and fix problems on the spot. Since I had a 20-minute transportation buffer before I affected the assembly plant, being down for a minute or two wasn't an issue.

This time, 10 or 15 minutes went by. Then the maintenance guy came up to me and said, "Hey, Ernie. This is pretty bad."

Now, you might say that as a new manager, I was a bit over-confident. I had started my career in Powertrain, and had developed the standards for most of the processes, so I figured the job would be relatively easy. There were some serious flaws in that thinking, of course, which we'll discuss later.

My response to the maintenance guy was therefore pretty typical.

"I know you're going to do your best to fix the problem," I said. "I'll call over and tell people we'll be a few minutes late. We'll be good."

At around the 20-minute mark, he came back and said, "This is a problem. Come. Let me show you."

I went over with him and had a look. The trouble area was where our conveyor line met the pallet conveyor. What had happened was a pallet had collided with the conveyor line, which then pulled it under the bottom, mangling up the conveyor in the process. There was actually a pallet trapped in the concrete pit underneath the conveyor. I asked him what it was going to take to fix it.

"Fix it? We haven't even gotten to where the problem is yet," he said.

That's the first time I got a funny feeling in my stomach that I wasn't going to get by with a simple machine breakdown—this was going to be much greater.

I said, "You know what? We're doing everything we can at this point." With our buffer now gone, we shut Trim One down in assembly, so now we had 50 or 60 people waiting for us. So we started getting a little entourage of people who had come into our area to take a look.

Six or seven minutes later, when Trim One's buffer had passed, we shut down Trim Two, affecting another 50 or 60 people, and then Trim Three. The little entourage had grown into a crowd, and I was getting all kinds of input from people in different functional areas. It was hard to toggle all those ideas at once and ensure maintenance had all the resources they needed.

Needless to say, I was extremely concerned and began pleading with the maintenance team member, "Come on now, I really don't want to shut the whole plant down."

After we were 45 minutes into this, our axle team had shut down the chassis lines. The incident had now left approximately

500 team members unable to run their production processes. Then came final assembly and other feeding departments, and in a little over an hour, we had shut down the entire plant.

From this point, cars were no longer coming off the line, so the outage was costing the company a lot of money per minute. Then, one by one, the vice presidents started showing up. My Japanese trainer was patiently coaching me, and my general manager and vice president were as well, but given my state of mind, I can't say I was very receptive with all that was happening around me.

Then I heard a voice from the background saying, "Mr. Cho is coming."

Now at this point, I felt that the last thing in the world I wanted was a visit from our president. This situation was far beyond anything I had ever experienced, and despite my years of training and conditioning in Toyota's culture, I began to fear the worst. I even found myself considering what I'd like to take home from my desk—I was actually thinking I should find a box and grab some stuff so I'd have it ready.

Mr. Cho's office was about a mile away from Powertrain. Instead of driving, he walked the whole way, and it seemed to take forever. "When will he get here? Let's get this over with," I thought. I was dreading facing him as I waited.

After about 20 minutes, Mr. Cho arrived in the building. The area coordinators went to the door to formally greet him and escort him to the area, as was the tradition.

When he arrived at our area, Mr. Cho looked carefully at our activity logs, kept by maintenance and production. Then he walked up to me, shook my hand, and said, "Ernie-san, do you have everything you need?"

I managed to answer, "Yes, we have everything we need. We've got the best maintenance team. We've got support from other shops coming over to help us as well. We have the best of the best here."

Then he said, "Thank you for shutting the plant down. We'll fix this problem."

Then he turned, chatted briefly with several other Powertrain managers, and then went back to the main plant.

A COMPLETELY DIFFERENT VIEW

**Russ Scaffede, former Vice President
and General Manager, Powertrain,
Toyota Motor Manufacturing Kentucky**

I'll never forget a speech Mr. Cho gave at a big automotive conference in the late 1980s. There were 400 or 500 people in the audience, and the big three all had vice presidents and executives there to talk. Everybody was talking about external factors such as emissions standards, the global economy, and what the government needed to do to help them be more competitive.

Then Mr. Cho got up, and he spoke for one hour about what Toyota does to support the production team members so that they can be more successful on the plant floor. Then we broke for lunch, and I'll never forget the buzz in the lunchroom. Everybody was saying, "Did you guys understand what just happened?" Here were all the automotive industries in America talking about what everybody's got to do to save them, and here's a Japanese guy in America explaining what they're doing to help the production team members be more successful. Everybody picked that up during that conversation. It was a completely different view of things.

A NEW TAKE ON LEADERSHIP

Some people might wonder why Mr. Cho would walk all the way to Powertrain to look at some logs and talk with me for 15 seconds. Somebody might think, "Why didn't he just call the executive coordinator for Powertrain and get the information he needed, and then call the production manager?"

The answer is that Mr. Cho didn't just see this incident as something that had to be fixed. He also saw an opportunity to have a positive influence on the company culture, and he wasn't going to pass it up. Here he had a very young production manager, a large audience, and a perfect situation for reinforcing a culture that says we stop and fix things. He could do one simple thing and make a big difference. He could walk to Powertrain, take his time, and show that our values must never be compromised, even in a very stressful time when we were shut down. And he could do it in a way that would really cause people to take note and remember the lesson.

Now a lot of people may have been thinking that Mr. Cho was coming to either reprimand or fire me. His actions showed how wrong that assumption was, and the visit had enormous impact on our culture, just as he had intended. People at TMMK still talk about that story many years later, and it profoundly changed the way I would manage people for the rest of my career.

So what some people might have thought was an unnecessary visit by Mr. Cho was actually a very efficient use of his time. When you consider all the efforts that go into "culture change" in many organizations—training courses, management retreats, consulting reports, etc.—the hour Mr. Cho invested here was a bargain for the company, and far more effective than any outside intervention.

Mr. Cho was an unusually successful leader even by Toyota standards, and his depth of vision influenced thousands of people. Where other managers might have merely seen a costly production delay, Mr. Cho saw a group of people who needed to be developed, and a perfect opportunity to do that. In our sessions today, we refer to acts of leadership like this as "Mr. Cho moments."

MANAGING VERSUS ENGAGING

**Russ Scaffede, former Vice President
and General Manager, Powertrain,
Toyota Motor Manufacturing Kentucky**

Toyota had a very different way of managing, and it was strongly focused on employee engagement. To understand the context, you have to go back and understand the years of built-up animosity and strained relationships between employees, union, and management in the Big Three. Essentially, there was an environment and a set of rules that made it impossible to engage employees.

There were many people at GM who understood this, including some of the best managers I've ever worked for, but around half the people, both on the labor and management side, were entrenched in the old ways and very unreceptive to change.

Toyota, on the other hand, was able to set up a system where it could engage its employees to foster identity with their jobs and continuous improvement. And because TMMK was a greenfield situation and NUMMI was a shuttered plant that Toyota had revitalized, the company was able to make sure that everybody was willing to go out and help the company improve.

So our job as leaders at TMMK wasn't about command and control—it was more about engaging than managing. This is not to say that the financials, the metrics, and the necessary reporting weren't considered critical. They were, but this was a small part of what we did.

DEVELOPING LEADERS FROM DAY ONE

Joining Toyota in 1988 as a team leader in Powertrain was the best career decision I ever made, but it didn't feel that way initially. Two weeks after my start date, I was on a plane to Chicago en route to Nagoya, Japan, with no idea of what I was going to learn, and definitely outside of my comfort zone. I even remember thinking when we landed in Chicago, "I could just get out here and come back home." I learned later that many of my colleagues were feeling that way.

When the company built its leadership team, it was not looking for car builders so much as people builders. I had worked for the past eight years at the nearby IBM plant, where I had started in entry-level assembly. I was fortunate to be promoted six levels, and had one level to go to reach the technician level, where I would progress from hourly to salaried employee. During that time, I had been given the opportunity to develop some leadership skills that I believe were of interest to my interviewers at Toyota.

IBM stressed many of the skills and values that are characteristic of Toyota. We were very conscious of process and continuous improvement, and there was a disciplined approach to identifying and solving problems. I had some excellent leaders and mentors as well, and the company had a vision for my long-term development and challenged me to meet that vision.

Toyota, however, practiced people development on a whole different level. From day one, it was made very clear that the company did not hire me to be a team leader for the rest of my life. My group leader wanted to know where I wanted to be in five years, where I wanted to be when I retired, and what it would take to get there. The understanding was that I would be willing to stretch myself to achieve my goals.

This thinking was very prevalent when I arrived in Japan and first met my trainer Mr. Shoichi Ikoma (Sho-san). He had a precise set of learning objectives for me during the trip, and he knew exactly how he wanted me to get there. He was very knowledgeable, and a hard worker who took his role as trainer very seriously. He spent a great deal of time with me, including many lunches and dinners. Also, as I later learned, he was being evaluated based on how successful he had made me.

The rest of the team leaders who had come over were in assembly, while I, being in Powertrain, was in the machine shop across the street. We went to work at the rear axle line, which was the line I would have at TMMK. The work was being done in an open area, and it was extremely hot, yet the people were all working without breaking a sweat. It all looked so easy. But when I got on the line for the first time, I thought, "Wow, this is more difficult than they make it look!"

The rear axle team had four processes. In that area, you could see all the way from the beginning, where they built the shaft up, connected it with knuckles or carriers, married the shock absorber to it, and then installed the spring and the upper support stud to mount into the vehicle.

What I found stunning is that they were completing these processes in 28 seconds. "How am I ever going to meet this expectation?" I wondered.

My trainer, however, knew exactly what I was thinking, what I had to learn, and how I could learn it most efficiently. He knew all the processes intimately. Initially we spent time on the mechanical parts, how they went together, and the sequence of the processes.

But mechanics and layouts were just the introduction—the real core of my training was around culture and people. My trainer understood the culture so well that he was able to break it to me gradually instead of throwing it at me all at once. After my orientation and a couple of days of getting to know the layout of the area, we began on my primary objective. I was to "master one process" thoroughly, which they referred to as my MOP.

The process he used was very similar to training within industry (TWI) or job instruction training (JIT). He would give me a very small piece of the process to start with, and then gradually start adding to it. Of course, I was there trying to make a big impression and often tried to do too much. He said, "Slow down. Slow down. Understand what you're doing before you do it." He was a very good teacher. And he was standing by me literally almost the whole time I was there. Needless to say, the company was very serious about me getting this right.

I am pleased to say that I got through the MOP in my second week, which allowed time for me to be developed further. My trainer then challenged me to come up with three improvement ideas for that process. As I found waste and developed ideas for improvements, he helped me do experiments to prove my ideas. This was my first exposure to changing a process.

Initially, I began to look for major gaps that would allow me to "hit a home run" by introducing a big process change. At that point, my trainer took me aside and said to me, "Home runs are OK, but we are looking for small improvements that add up to big change." He instructed me to take it slow and prove each idea before I moved on to the next.

Out of that emerged my best idea—a way to provide a little bit of flexibility between two processes that would make it easier to recover and maintain flow if a small abnormality occurred. It was a small idea, but after my trainer and I had worked on it and done the experiments, it was pretty solid.

Then he did something that stuck with me throughout my entire career. He brought the team together—the people doing the actual work—and had me present my idea to them. So here I was talking to people with as much as 15 years of experience. I was nervous, to say the least.

I presented my idea through a Japanese interpreter and then asked for feedback. The reaction surprised me. The team not only listened and took my idea seriously, but began to give suggestions about how that idea could be made even better. They were very supportive—it was like, "What if we do this? What if we do that?"

We then tested the improvements together. I believe that my original idea would have saved two seconds, but by the time

the team had given feedback, we had doubled that to four seconds. I was then amazed by the teamwork they displayed as we
implemented my improved idea.

After the improvement was in place, the plant manager
came to the area, and once again I presented the idea. While I
spoke, the whole team stood around me as a show of support.
The plant manager then congratulated me on my idea, and told
me that this was the start of my journey, and that I must never
forget the power of people. What an impact this had on a one-
month-old Kentucky team leader!

LEARNING THROUGH EXPERIENCE

John Shook, Chairman and CEO,
Lean Enterprise Institute

Taking hundreds of people to Japan for three weeks or more was
a huge expense and effort. Many of the team leaders and group
leaders had never been overseas. Many had to scramble to obtain
their first passport just in time to make the trip! Some got a little
homesick, and others struggled with the food, not to mention the
language, of course. But almost all found the three weeks working
alongside their counterparts in Toyota City to be a life-changing
experience. Seeing is believing, and there is no substitute for the
actual physical experience of working on a Toyota assembly line.

THE JOURNEY CONTINUES

The plant manager was right about the start of the journey part.
There were many aspects of this lesson that would be apparent
at various points in my career and would be critical to my role
as a leader.

As I realized later on, my trainer was trying to connect me to the True North from day one. This was why he took me to the assembly line and showed me where the axles went on, all the different components of the axles and how they were assembled, and how they were connected in the assembly line. What he wanted me to understand was "they are my customer, and I've got to do everything I can to make my customer happy."

When he wanted me to master a process, the real objective was helping me to understand what a process looks like to a team member. It was all about what the team members are feeling when they're on the line. Then he would ask, "What are you thinking?" It was all about gauging where I was at with the culture piece.

Back in Kentucky, the development continued. We didn't have our machines yet, so I spent two weeks on the wheel and tire line helping to develop standards for processes that I had absolutely nothing to do with. The whole idea was for me to start understanding how to develop standardized work, and how to look at process flow. It didn't matter whose department the work was in!

After the equipment arrived and we began to set up our actual processes, it became clear that things weren't exactly as they had been in Japan. Instead of just following a template, we had to use our newly developed skills to help set up and test the processes. We got a lot of things wrong, of course, but we knew where we were going, and were beginning to understand the "why." That's when the wisdom behind that training really started to make sense.

The presence of our Japanese trainers, however, remained very strong throughout our start-up of production in 1988, and for several years after that. As we discussed in earlier chapters, these trainers included some of Toyota's best people, and their knowledge and mentoring skills were phenomenal. They had an intrinsic knack of grasping where we were in our journey with regard to the Toyota Production System (TPS) and other PDCA thinking processes.

As I got more confident with the basics, they began to spend more time coaching me on developing my subordinates, who were, according to the servant leadership model, the people I worked for. The idea was that management isn't about "knowing and telling," it is, as we discussed in previous chapters, about "leading and learning" simultaneously. Along similar lines, I often mention to organizations that we have to condition ourselves to refrain from "telling, selling, and convincing," but instead practice "engaging, involving, and empowering" people.

As I recall those early days with the Japanese trainers, they were always present in the background, observing, assessing, calculating, and waiting for opportunities to intervene with questions that led to specific coaching points. It wasn't uncommon in the beginning for a trainer to stop me for a couple of minutes in between production and trials and ask, "What was your thinking when you made that decision, Ernie-san?"

Then I would discuss with him the reasons behind my thinking. Sometimes he agreed with me, and sometimes we had further discussions. At first, I thought that he was "double-checking" my answers to ensure the right decisions were made that maintained our team KPIs. Later, I realized that this wasn't about second-guessing my work, but about the long-term journey and laying the foundation for continuous learning.

Often at the end of each day we would summarize what had taken place. Where I didn't meet expectations, we would have a "plan versus actual" type of discussion. The conversation frequently involved people, and the trainer would often ask me questions like, "Who did you develop today, and how did you do it?" or, "What did you both learn?" He ended the huddle with, "What do you see as the next step of your own development?" Then we would have very open and honest communication, and set a plan for raising my own bar of knowledge and preparing me for all the obstacles and challenges that might arise.

As time went on, these discussions became less frequent as he confirmed that my skill was improving. My trainer was involving and engaging me with what he was taught years ago and passing this knowledge on to me, which was referred to as sharing our wisdom. We both knew he couldn't hold my hand forever, so he transferred as much knowledge as possible and let us fail occasionally on purpose so we would learn.

There were many lessons. I learned to understand that failure leads to successes—I just had to be patient enough to see the greater purpose behind the lesson. I learned that frequent and honest communication with your team members gives you the opportunity to develop them and yourself simultaneously. I was encouraged to learn something about each one of my team members to help build mutual trust and respect. I continue to practice this even today.

PEOPLE DEVELOPMENT IN PERSPECTIVE

Pete Gritton, former Vice President of Human Resources, Toyota Engineering and Manufacturing, North America

I was the ninth American hired at TMMK and came on board in November of 1986 as an employee relations manager. I'd been in HR for about 15 years, and figured it was my job to convince these Japanese that they were in America now, and we do things differently here.

We started out by writing the policies. The process was very simple. We had a policy review meeting every Thursday evening at 7:00. My job was to bring in a policy recommendation and present it, talk through it, and hopefully get approval. My audience, by the way, were some of the smartest people I'd ever worked with.

I wanted to have a success on my first night, so I picked overtime pay. I was going to dazzle them with my presentation and get quick approval and then take on more challenging things later. Overtime pay was the most straightforward thing I could think of. I was proposing very basic things like time and a half for over 40 hours.

I presented my policy, and Nate, my boss, asked, "Why?" Now, I'd never actually thought about that, but I was an experienced human resource professional, so I started talking anyway. I explained that basically everybody does this.

"Ah, okay," he said, "so we're only going to do stuff that everybody does?"

I knew I was in trouble, but I started talking again and used a whole lot of words, and explained that our employees expected it, and if we didn't, they'd be upset.

"Oh, okay," said Nate, "so we're only going to do things that our employees expect us to do? We won't challenge them, or ask them to think or do things differently?"

This process went on for six weeks. Every week he would ask me why, and I would go back and investigate the whys. I was spending so much time on the whys that I never got a chance to change the policy at all. On the sixth week, Nate suddenly put up his hand and said, "Okay, we'll do it," and signed off on the policy that I had recommended the first week.

So the process wasn't about the policy—it was about helping me understand two critical points. One was that Toyota has a unique business model that has been very successful, and everything has to be aligned with that. It may not always be what people expect, but this is what we are doing to drive success for both the company and the employees.

The second thing he was trying to teach me is that you can't make assumptions and speculations at Toyota without doing your homework. "Well, this is normal practice" is not acceptable. We have to have fact-based decision making that has logic and facts and data involved in it. When we make conclusions about things and recommend them, we need to confirm that it's really well thought out, deeply researched, and the right fit for us.

This was one of those "Oh my gosh, what have I gotten myself into" kinds of moments. But it was also very exciting because it was really resonating with me, and when I thought about it, it all made perfect sense. I had just not been exposed to that sophisticated a level of thinking about the role of human resources in a company.

THE DUTY TO HELP OTHERS SUCCEED

I became manager of Powertrain through a series of promotions, from team leader to group leader to assistant manager of Engine Assembly and Machining, and then back to Powertrain Axle as manager. What I found was that the basic principles I applied in my daily work hadn't changed one iota—the difference was that I was spending more and more of my time making other people successful.

There were always people to mentor me and coach me as a manager, and they were as eager for me to succeed as I was. In our system, my success was their most important measure. In turn, they knew that my success depended on my subordinates, so they taught me how to develop them. When I became manager of Powertrain, I was teaching people to develop their subordinates. It was a little like a pyramid system for developing better people!

As the story with Mr. Cho illustrates, developing people usually took precedence over particular situations, and we had to be reminded of this sometimes. I remember a situation where my trainer told me that a worker on the line was struggling with some personal issues, and that this was impacting his work.

"You should go and talk with him," he said.

"Sorry, I can't do that now," I said, "I've got a severe problem in assembly to deal with."

My trainer then asked, "What's more important than developing your people?"

Message received. But that wasn't the last time I had to be reminded, and I was often reminding my leadership team as well.

When I actually did go to respond to a severe incident on the line, the priority of developing people didn't change. Instead of applying my Powertrain knowledge and saying, "Do this, and then this," I would be coaching my assistant manager to coach the specialist to develop a strategy for fixing that problem. Once again, solving the problem is important, but so is engaging people in solving the problem themselves so they can someday replace the leaders that are coaching them.

Our development strategy was for every single person to move up two levels in the organization. After I had moved from production to HR, for example, I knew that if I hired an entry-level administrative assistant, I had to be thinking from day one what skills this worker would need to become a specialist. This meant I might have to rebalance people's workload to make sure they got the range of experience that they would need later on, or include them in projects that weren't directly relevant to their daily work. This required patience, and often putting minor problems on hold, but we constantly focused and refocused on this.

So essentially, I would spend my days trying to work myself out of a job. Of course, I knew that if I made others successful, that meant I was successful as well. Trust was a big factor here—I knew that Toyota was not the kind of company that would counsel me to teach others my job and then let me go because I was no longer needed. Unfortunately, some companies today do just that, tearing down their culture in the process.

I have to admit, however, that there was some tugging at the ego when people started to use their newly acquired skills to change the processes that I had created. I got a strong reminder of this soon after I had retired and first went to TMMK as a visitor. When I got to my former work area, I noticed that managers I had helped move up had made a lot of changes to the processes I had put in place. "Wait a moment, that's mine," I thought. But then I realized that it was not mine, it was theirs. They were being super successful, and it was a great feeling to see that. And today, I have to admit that those processes, as I had initially developed them, wouldn't survive today.

MINE VERSUS OURS

A key aspect to helping people move up is encouraging them to share what they know in the form of improved standards. This in a sense makes them dispensable in their current role, but at the same time, more valuable to the company because of the deeper knowledge and understanding they've acquired.

Few organizations think this way. I believe the base assumption in many situations is that when people are in a position, they will be there forever, and there's no need for anybody else to know the details of how they get their job done. If they leave the company, well, we'll deal with it then.

Of course, "then" is too late. I was at a plant not long ago for a client, and we were discussing a woman who had worked in payroll and HR for 36 years. She was very good at what she did, and had accumulated a great deal of what I call tribal knowledge—tricks of the trade that she used to do her job successfully. However, since she was in her seventies, there was a good chance she might want to retire soon, and that tribal knowledge would go out the door forever. I asked them what their plans were for that.

"Oh my gosh, we'd pay her more to stay," was the answer.

I reminded them that money might not be the deciding factor for her, and challenged them to come up with ideas for capturing the tribal knowledge that this woman had accumulated.

Furthermore, if we can get this worker to a place where she's learning new concepts and skills as opposed to applying the same old knowledge, we have a better chance of retaining her. As my trainer told me early on in my career, the minute you quit learning is the minute your value starts going down.

Now, the accumulation of tribal knowledge is a big problem in most organizations, and often, people have no desire to share it. If I view my coworkers as competitors, why would I want to show them something that would help them become as good as or better than me? This happens on an individual level, or on a larger scale, where sales won't share their data with marketing, or manufacturing with R&D. This is how we get siloed bureaucracies where "the left hand doesn't know what the right hand is doing."

I believe that tribal knowledge actually harms the company for several reasons. First of all, it's not sustainable, as the example with the woman in payroll shows. Secondly, because it's not out there to be challenged and improved, it tends to create an inflexible "this is the way we do things around here" mindset.

Worst of all, tribal knowledge perpetuates a culture where people don't work as a team toward common goals. Where openly shared knowledge brings people together, tribal knowledge creates barriers.

Therefore, we must harvest our tribal knowledge by encouraging people to share their ideas, and when these are proven valid, incorporate them into our standards. That way, the full power of these "knacks, experiences, and feels" gets fully realized throughout the organization and passed on to the next generation.

I internalized this fairly early on, mainly because of the way I was treated by the company. When I saw how generous my trainers were in sharing their knowledge and ideas, it was natural to follow suit. So as a leader, I never hesitated to share my knowledge, whether helping a subordinate get to my level of knowledge, giving another department a hand with a problem, or sharing successful practices with suppliers.

Of course, in an environment that encourages the sharing of ideas, we also need clear guidelines for evaluating and improving them. In addition to developing people, we need to make sure that they understand how to develop their ideas according to the needs of the company and the company's stakeholders. We'll look at that in the next chapter.

12

Aligning People and Purpose

■ ■ ■

L eaders at Toyota, as we have seen, play a key role in pro-
moting a very special way of thinking throughout the
organization. To many people, this will seem counterintuitive. Senior leaders, some would argue, should delegate culture
to others, and instead spend their time trying to influence the
"big picture" issues such as cost of sales, customer satisfaction,
and market share.

One of the problems with that approach is that traditional
indicators that we see in a company's financials are lagging
indicators. It's mandatory to track and report these in terms of
advising investors and government regulators, but as we discussed in Chapter 9, they have very limited value in helping
us improve. Managing based on what already happened is, as
Deming observed, like managing through the rearview mirror—
by the time we become aware of a problem, it's often too late.

Leaders at Toyota focused their day-to-day work on leading indicators that could be followed in real time—the factors

they could influence proactively. They fulfilled their fiduciary responsibility around the traditional indicators, of course, but even at the highest levels, they didn't spend a great deal of time on this.

A good example of this is how companies monitor customer satisfaction. If "customer sat" is down in a traditional company, senior managers might learn about this in a quarterly report. At this point, the problem will be well-entrenched, putting pressure on decision makers to act immediately. However, with no understanding of when, where, and how their processes are producing at a given point, they can only guess at root causes, keeping them in perpetual firefighting mode.

At Toyota, on the other hand, we constantly monitored leading indicators that could be seen not in a financial report, but in the workplace. We all knew, for example, that on-time delivery is a strong contributor to customer satisfaction, so we monitored that every day.

If on-time delivery wasn't where it should have been, we would identify the gap, find the root causes, and engage our people in improving the standard work in order to close that gap. And if there was no gap, as we learned earlier, we sometimes created one by raising the bar.

This thinking applied everywhere. Whether the problem or improvement opportunity was in production, R&D, sales, or customer service, we knew that at the end of the day, it was up to our people to move the needle and make us better.

The most important leading indicator, therefore, is the readiness of people at the *gemba* to make improvements. If Mr. Cho walked into an area and saw that people were connected with the True North and engaged in solving problems and creating improvements as a team, he knew that this would contribute to higher customer satisfaction, lower production costs, and ultimately, a sustainable future for the company. If he saw a morale problem, or a leader not showing respect for people, he knew there was a gap that had to be addressed immediately.

In a nutshell, this is why developing people is the most effective long-term business strategy, and why our executives made this their, and our, most important priority.

WALKING THE TALK

Leading indicators share one important characteristic—they are all visible at the *gemba*. Therefore, it was common for leaders at all levels to spend considerable time watching processes in our plants.

Our leaders, therefore, did *gemba* walks frequently. In contrast with the common idea that a workplace visit is about "management going on a tour," this was a disciplined process where managers had objectives going in and paid significant due diligence to ensure that they were viewing the right indicators, asking the right questions, and providing help where people needed it.

The *gemba* walk always began with "why." Each time, we would ask ourselves questions like:

- What value am I adding to the organization by going to the *gemba*?
- Am I removing barriers that might prevent people from doing their work most effectively and efficiently?
- Am I providing resources and guidance where needed to help people be successful in problem solving?

We always kept in mind three pillars that defined the basic mindset of the *gemba* walk: reinforcing True North, monitoring KPI boards, and observing and assisting with problem-solving and improvement activity. Figure 12.1, which I use with our clients, shows how these are interrelated.

The True North aspect of these visits was all about reinforcing everybody's line of sight to the customer. We weren't

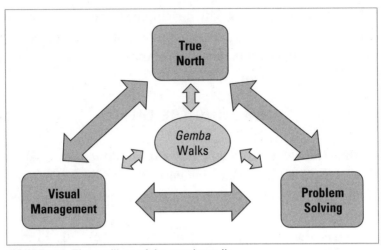

FIGURE 12.1 Three pillars of the *gemba* walk

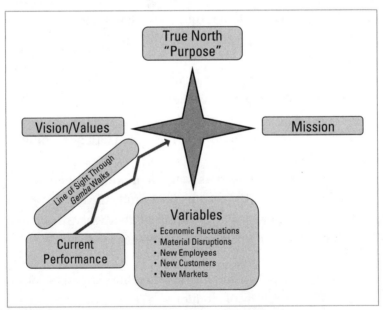

FIGURE 12.2 Connecting the daily work with True North

stressing the "get your daily output" idea that is so common in executive visits—instead, we were helping people appreciate how each worker contributes to customer satisfaction, to the company's long-term success, and to making Toyota a positive factor in society. This interaction played a key role in helping team members appreciate the "why" behind their work and the continuous improvement of their processes. Figure 12.2 illustrates how we focused our efforts in order to help people visualize these connections.

A vitally important aspect of this was showing presence. It's one thing to issue a memo from Human Resources telling how important a team member is to the success of the company, and quite another to have a senior manager show up at the *gemba*, ask a worker "How's your process?" and then engage in a productive dialogue on how to improve the company. No matter how high we rose in the organization, we never became strangers to the *gemba*.

CONNECTING WITH PEOPLE

Senior Operations Manager, Aerospace

Ernie and Tracey's coaching on A3 problem solving helped our team tremendously. They certainly helped us to improve our problem-solving capability from a technical standpoint. More important, they helped us better understand the change management element of problem solving. They challenged us to build real partnerships with team members on the floor, to listen to them and to share our thoughts with them, ultimately building trust and credibility.

Ernie modeled these relational skills each time we went to the factory floor to work actual problems. My team members were very impressed with Ernie's ability to quickly connect with people and to get them engaged. He might start the conversation asking about the hat or the shirt that they were wearing. He would find a way to steer the conversation into something that mattered to the person and get him or her to open up. In most cases, it would turn into a meaningful dialogue very quickly, and we would gain valuable new insights into the problem we were attacking.

On the floor, we carefully reviewed all the leading indicators. This was achieved with the help of visual management tools, which make all standards, targets, and actual conditions highly visible in the workplace so that everyone can see and understand the actual conditions versus the requirements. Thus, we looked at the KPI boards to study lead times, material flows, defects, safety incidents, and other metrics. We looked at indicators in the green, yellow, and red areas on our boards and noted how long they had been there. We looked at continuous flow and reviewed posted work standards, training schedules, Quality Circles, suggestions turned in, A3s in progress, and other posted documents.

Equally important, we watched the processes themselves—an activity that my trainer called "seeing through the process." Here, the objective was to see the process through the team members' eyes and to understand what happens when you are not watching.

This involved asking a lot of questions, either of ourselves or of the people. Were there signs of undue strain? Were people waiting? Could we see unnecessary steps or other forms of waste?

The personal side was vital, and was never left out. Did people seem satisfied with their work process and environment? Did they relate well and support each other? Were their team leader and group leader showing respect for them? It takes many visits to the *gemba* to be able to understand these questions.

Understanding the problems at the *gemba*, and how workers were solving them, was intimately related to the other two pillars. When we asked about problem solving or sat in on *kaizen* activities, we were always acutely aware of the indicators and of the "why" behind an improvement based on the True North.

I believe that GTS[6], which we described in Part 2, really summarizes what we were doing on our *gemba* walks. We lived by Taiichi Ohno's words that there are always problems, and were always Going to See to discover them. We Grasped the Situation in order to gather the facts and avoid premature conclusions based on assumptions and tribal knowledge. We practiced Get to Solution when we looked at the teamwork behind improvement and how well change was being communicated.

We practiced Get to Standardization and constantly asked whether our standards truly served the need of our company. We considered how economic fluctuations, materials disruptions, or new employees might disrupt our processes, and practiced Get to Sustainability to find ways to ensure that they remained stable. And finally, applying the idea of Get to Stretch, we challenged our workers to raise the bar.

THE MEANING OF TRUE NORTH

Mike Hoseus, former Assistant General Manager of Operations and HR at Toyota Motor Manufacturing Kentucky, Executive Director, The Center for Quality People and Organizations.

I think the big challenge for companies is leveraging this idea of True North so that there's a strong awareness at the team member level of the company's purpose. The role of the team members is not to do their job, but to improve their job, so there has to be a context for that. Leaders have to understand that and get the supervisors to train that role.

When I talk with companies about this, I say, "It's where your numbers are," that is, you want to have the bulk of your employees actively pulling the organization forward toward the company's purpose. But most managers are caught up in running the business, but not improving it, and the idea of companywide engagement doesn't really register.

When I ask people the purpose of their business, they say "to make money." And then I ask, "Is that really going to touch people's hearts and minds?"

Of course, Toyota never apologized for making money, but the True North was different from that. "We're the most profitable car company on earth," they say, "but that's not our purpose." The purpose is to create long-term mutual prosperity for all stakeholders, and making money allows us to do that.

When we were at TMMK, it had our hearts and minds, and I truly believed that what was good for the company was good for me, and vice versa. And that's what I focus on when I talk with organizations about True North.

STRATEGY BASED ON LEADING INDICATORS

Working toward improving the leading indicators at the *gemba* wasn't just a method of supporting the company's strategy. It actually *was* the strategy.

Hoshin kanri is, to simplify, the collaborative process for designing and deploying the goals and objectives that constitute management policy. The name is quite significant. *Hoshin* is Japanese for "policy, plan, purpose, or target," while *kanri* represents the phrase *nichijo kanri*, which means "daily, normal, or regular."

The name reflects how we deployed strategy. Unlike a fixed strategy that we would be stuck with for a year, our *hoshin* was continually monitored and revised based on results against leading indicators, and through interaction with people at the *gemba*. Essentially, PDCA thinking applied to our *hoshins* as it applied to everything else we did.

A *hoshin*, therefore, is never an end in itself. We didn't go in and say, "How do we develop our *hoshin* to meet the company's *hoshin*," for example. The question was always, "How do we develop a *hoshin* to meet our needs?" based on our past experiences and our understanding. The point is that when you're aligned with the True North, what you need is exactly what the company needs.

Hoshin kanri was a way of life for us. We didn't wait until the end of the year to develop our *hoshins*—we were developing and evolving them all year long. We would look at our indicators, track important ones on our visual boards, utilize the boards to see our gaps, and then make sure we were always moving the needle forward. I can't emphasize enough how much we were conditioned to use leading indicators to predict results instead of waiting for them. There will always be some of both, of course, but leading helps us to manage the problem so that the problem doesn't manage us.

Ongoing dialogue was also very important, and a very central aspect of *hoshin kanri* was something we called "catch-ball"—a metaphor to describe informal back-and-forth conversation between leaders and people in the processes at the *gemba*. This helped us learn whether our thinking was correct, how and what we were tracking daily, and if there were any gaps. It also helped us build trust by showing the workers we depended on that we valued their input and were truly listening. Policies didn't "come out of the blue" at Toyota—we worked very hard to keep everybody on the same page regardless of people's level in the organization.

Now, you'd think that as a manager, developing the *hoshin kanri* itself was something I would absolutely insist on doing myself, but actually, that wasn't the case. It was my responsibility, but it was also an excellent opportunity to give my specialist and assistant managers an understanding of our needs and how to develop around these needs at a higher level. So in many cases, I let them do the work, and I have to say, they did an awesome job.

Similarly, my leaders gave me the opportunity to work on their *hoshins*, so I got some exposure to planning at a very senior level.

PURSUING HIGH LEVEL OBJECTIVES

Al Mason, Vice President, Operational Excellence, Altra Industrial Motion

We've been applying problem solving in some very strategic areas. Revenue has grown pretty dramatically, but most of this has been through acquisitions. So we have been working on a sustained campaign to improve our organic growth. Now, this is a huge problem, with many causes and influences.

Our senior management has been concerned about organic growth, that is, growth other than through acquisitions. First, we had the traditional response—things like "I know what the issue is, we just need to restructure the sales organization this way, and that will solve all of the problems."

But in the dialogue that I had with our CEO, the conclusion was that we have to go and see and then break down this problem, because it's very complex, with a lot of contributing factors. So we decided to pick a business unit, go deep in understanding the drivers of organic growth, and then share what we learned with other business units.

So this is part of a big change in our management thinking in the past couple of years, and it's really exciting to see our leaders thinking that way rather than jumping to "Here's what we need to do." And I'd say 90 percent of this has come from our sessions with Tracey and Ernie.

RAISING THE BAR COMPANYWIDE

One of the key outcomes of the *hoshin kanri* exercise is that it introduced strategic goals into the workplace. Here, we were creating gaps, which were then addressed through strategic A3s, which we introduced in Chapter 10.

For example, let's say that based on the president's *hoshin kanri*, we have a companywide objective to increase productivity by 5 percent. The way we view this is that there is now a 5 percent gap between where we are currently and where we need to be. We would then use the A3 process to create a strategy for closing that gap.

With high-level gaps, you need to account for variations within the organization. Some shops might have already made some progress on improving their productivity, and you might not want to ask them for the full 5 percent improvement. Other shops might need to improve much more, or, to state that differently, might have larger opportunities for improvement, and you might want to ask them for 6 percent or 7 percent.

An individual shop would then look at their assigned gap(s), break down the problem, and prioritize the best opportunities for closing that gap. An individual department might have dozens of A3s aimed toward different aspects of this, and might arrive at solutions such as rebalanced workloads, improved standards, training, or revised equipment layout or configuration.

The president, however, was not the only person setting our *hoshin* strategies. As the manager in Powertrain, I would have a *hoshin* level board in the department that displayed our connection to those goals, and the two or three prioritized items that I had identified in my department based upon looking at the processes, results, and, you guessed it, leading indicators.

The *hoshin* goals we got from the president were often already aligned with our departments. The point here is that when you're doing *hoshin* or strategy deployment correctly, you become very aware of your leading indicators. You know where you have to make improvement, and you are going to see gaps cascading upward and downward through all the *hoshin* levels.

It's also important to remember that we were always asking, "What are we capable of?" Anything less than what was achievable always meant that there were gaps to be filled, and we didn't wait for any annual objectives to bring them out into the open and address them.

So we would already have our own goals set, in many cases, before we would get the company goals and objectives. The company objectives would help us reflect on whether we might have missed something, but usually, they were less stringent than what we were already planning to do.

Our senior managers were also very realistic about what we could achieve. You wouldn't have 50 objectives—you would have five or six, and no more than 10. The expectation, of course, was that we intended to be successful with every one of them.

TOYOTA'S UNIQUE STRENGTHS

Pete Gritton, former Vice President of Human Resources, Toyota Engineering and Manufacturing, North America

If you compare Toyota's culture with other companies, there are two really significant strengths. One is the tremendous amount of alignment. Toyota really has everybody on the same page—there's a strong sense of one message, one voice. Most other organizations are leader-dominated because there is no culture to sustain and drive the behavior.

Along with that consistent direction is a tremendous development process where we're all getting developed in our thinking ways, in our behaviors. We're all getting the same consistent development in how we solve problems, which is the real meat of how we do improvement. This drives all these wonderful behaviors, and it keeps us all connected, and it keeps us all with the right priorities. We know today what our focus should be on. We have targets set every year, obviously with the *hoshin kanri* process and all that kind of stuff, but we always understand what's important and what's not.

The other big area is that the focus at Toyota is always on the people who produce the product that somebody's going to pay us for. So we're always focused on those team members in our production areas, and how we can help them be successful, and we have very clear roles and expectations for supporting these people.

This means that if we are in administrative functions like HR, finance, or senior management, we need to see ourselves in a support role, and with that come questions we have to always consider. Is our work aligned with the company's goals and targets? Are we cost effective, and doing everything we can to minimize unnecessary work that our customers would not willingly pay for? And are we minimizing the administrative burden on our suppliers, or our internal customers? These are questions that most companies don't consider.

A NEW PERSPECTIVE

Perhaps my biggest surprise in my career came when my leaders informed me that I was being moved out of the plant environment into HR. I had been very successful in my current role, and felt I had a deep knowledge of the processes, the equipment, and the people. On the other hand, HR was an area I knew little about.

I shouldn't have been surprised. The fact that I had grown comfortable in my role was a sign that it was time to raise the bar in my career and give me a new challenge. I knew all that, of course, but initially, it was small consolation. I was way out-side of my comfort zone.

Now, as you've seen, every leader at TMMK was involved in many of the traditional functions of HR, such as training, coaching, listening to personal concerns and issues, and help-ing people develop their career paths. Our work was about developing the best long-term policies to, essentially, support our number one objective of developing people. Consequently, when we looked at HR policies such as benefits, attendance, job transfers, and corrective actions, we always looked at these pol-icies from the viewpoint of the employee.

STEPPING INTO A CRISIS

Pete Gritton, former Vice President of Human Resources, Toyota Engineering and Manufacturing, North America

At a certain point, TMMK got big enough to support an on-site pharmacy, so that employees could get their nonemergency pre-scriptions filled on-site. So we set up this drugstore, if you will, in the back of a building, with a drive-through window and the whole works. Of course, we didn't want to run a drugstore, so we contracted with a company that did that sort of thing. The reps assured us that they'd done this hundreds of times, and there was nothing we had to worry about.

On the Monday we launched, I got a call from Ernie at about 3:30 or 4:00. "You've got to get over here," he said. "We've got dozens of people lined up in the lobby waiting on prescriptions, and cars are backed up all the way to the main highway."

What was happening was there was a flood of people want-ing to change over from Walgreens to Toyota Pharmacy, and they wanted to get their prescriptions filled. And of course, this was all happening at the end of people's shifts. So the whole system had shut down, and there were a lot of angry people.

Ernie and I were the two HR managers who were responsible for this, and in our world, we had failed by not doing more due diligence with the provider. There was not a darned thing we could do about the problem on that day, but we had to see this firsthand, and more important, we had to be able to look our people in the eye and say, "Yes, we screwed this up. This is a disaster, and we've got a lot of work to do to get it fixed."

Working in HR, I had many opportunities to apply the lessons I had learned as a manager in a new light. We used the same tools to solve problems, only the gaps were different. Where I would have been looking at a gap of a few seconds in a process in the shop, I might have been looking at a gap such as our insurance costs, or the cost of running our medical clinics. It was exciting to see how well the basics of continuous improvement and problem solving worked outside of the production environment.

As I got settled in HR, I was profoundly influenced by a lesson I had learned very early on when I first became a group leader. That all began when we hired a new team member into my department. It was always a special occasion to introduce new members to the team and share with them the standards that were expected of the team in order to make our internal and external customers happy.

During the first few months of his six-month evaluation period, the new team member progressed well and was an engaged and involved member in Quality Circles and our suggestion system. However, as the evaluation period progressed, I noticed that his performance and behavior were starting to decline. He began to miss work frequently, and his body language suggested a lack of engagement or enthusiasm expressed in the previous months.

I became concerned as to what in his attitude had changed. I thought to myself, "He should understand the expectations and standards, we have covered that in detail in his assimilation process." Unfortunately, I had to resort to our corrective action process to reinforce the standards and request countermeasure activity from him. My intention was to be a resource and guide for him through this, while making it clear that he needed to take ownership of his actions.

As I started the corrective action process as established by HR, I began to hear from other team members in the area that this individual really wasn't interested in working at Toyota (TMMK). His reason for being there, he had told people, was family pressure. This meant that he wasn't allowed to quit, but if he got fired, the pressure would be off him. My thinking at the time was, "If that is what he wants, I will help him out."

After working through the progressive levels of the corrective action process, it became time to recommend termination. The actual termination had to be signed off on by a senior executive. Working with my HR representative, I completed the proper paperwork that documented all of the steps I had taken. After completing the process, I went to the meeting with the senior executive for the sign-off.

In this meeting, I presented all the previous actions that had taken place to get to this point. I actually felt relieved that this would soon be over. It had consumed a lot of my time and energy over a few weeks.

The executive reviewed all the proper human resources documents, then looked up at me and said, "Ernie-san, have you done everything possible to make this person successful?"

I quickly answered, "Yes sir, I have," thinking I had helped this employee get what he wanted, and this would soon be one less issue on my plate.

He then responded in a way that was very unexpected to me and ultimately changed the way I thought about managing and mentoring people from that day forward.

He grabbed his pen and signed the termination documents, and as he handed them back to me, he looked me in the eye and said, "Ernie-san, you have failed."

He then went on to explain that any time we lose an employee, it is a loss for the company. As a servant leader, it was my responsibility to engage and understand each team member's learning style and what team members might need to develop into future leaders for the company. When that does not happen, everyone loses.

I was reminded that we have an investment in each person we hire, and when people become part of our team, we make a strong commitment to do everything possible to make them successful. We develop the thinking of each team member, expecting he or she will be a future leader.

EVERYBODY MEANS EVERYBODY

The takeaway from that lesson is that when we say "everybody matters," we really mean it, and we never give up on people and their development. It's awfully easy as a manager to brand somebody as a troublemaker and either neutralize the person's disruptive activity or, as people say, "get him off the bus." I'm grateful for learning how wrong this thinking was very early on, as it transformed how I manage for the better.

This caused me to realize, for example, that you can't just manage by looking at work processes alone. You have to reach out and make personal connections, and in the process, you begin to empathize with people and understand what it's like to be in their shoes. That's where you appreciate the real depth of how they see their work, how they relate to their coworkers, and how they feel about the company.

As well, this is how we develop the level of trust needed for employees to share their knowledge and ideas, support their team members, and dedicate themselves to the goals of the company. As mentioned, I developed this trust very early on because my trainers connected with me, even outside of working hours. There was never any question that I was important to Toyota, not just as a worker, but as a person.

My human relations skills have served me well in my current role as a trainer. In our sessions, we sometimes find a person who is having a tough time accepting the concepts that we are presenting. Some will raise a hand and state an objection, but often, the resistance will only be visible in their body language or facial expressions—signs that I learned to read over the years by connecting with team members on the line.

When I see that somebody is not coming along, it is ingrained in my being that we will not leave that person behind. Even when other participants say, "Don't listen to him, he's just a whiner," I will engage with that person, either during the session, during break, or at lunch afterward.

A good example is the senior level manager we discussed in Part 2 who objected to the idea that gaps must always be defined with real numbers based on real data. The difficulty was that the idea of looking for quantitative measurements for some aspects of his work was clearly drawing him outside of his comfort zone.

We spent 45 minutes on this during the session, which had a packed agenda as it was, but it was worth it. I find that many of the people who show some initial resistance become the strongest supporters of the concepts we teach.

This really encapsulates the "Everybody" behind E^3— Everybody Everyday Engaged. We really mean everybody!

THE FACTOR THAT MATTERS MOST

People love to ask questions like "What is the secret of management?" and I am often asked what the single most important aspect of management is. I say, without hesitation, it's about building trust.

As a servant leader, we accept that our success depends totally on what our people do out of their own free will. If they don't trust our leadership and willingly follow us, we are not real leaders. On the other hand, trust helps us build a win-win relationship where managers and workers are no more than two human beings working together toward a common goal.

To fulfill that trust, we look after people's interests by helping them advance in their careers. As a leader, I constantly have to be thinking, "How can I help this person advance to the highest level in the organization that he or she is capable of?" This isn't just about vague ideas—we are constantly working on concrete steps that will lead people toward achieving their potential.

The beauty of this is that when we constantly strive to make people successful, we get great results as well. But the biggest success of all is seeing people that have found success thanks to your efforts, and knowing you have made the kind of difference that really matters.

The journey for me has been priceless, and has taken me far beyond machines, production methods, and seconds on the clock. I have enjoyed the privilege of playing a significant role in the success of others, not just in their job, but personally. Best of all, I've then watched them turn around and do the same for others. They trusted me, they followed my leadership, and they used the same wisdom I had acquired to help others.

As a leader, you can make a lot of money, and a lot of leaders do that. But the legacy that you leave is the impact you have on people. Money can't buy the kind of satisfaction that this brings.

13

Reflections

■ ■ ■

Afew hours before Hurricane Matthew hit the U.S. coast, Tracey and I (Ernie) were driving home to Ormond Beach, Florida, on Interstate 75. As we stared at the solid white line of opposing headlamps, it felt very unsettling to be one of very few cars heading south, right into the hurricane.

The people in those cars must have wondered what we were thinking. Our biggest concern was for Tracey's parents, who had been forced to evacuate their home and were staying at our place. We also have neighbors on both sides that didn't have family close by to support them. We also felt we needed to protect our home. All in all, we were thinking how we'd feel if we didn't go and then regretted it.

In hindsight, I think our Toyota conditioning played a role here. Whenever there was a severe incident on the line, we would drop everything and help each other. It was second nature for us to head toward the crisis, not away from it, even if we weren't sure what the consequences would be.

The day before, in consultation with our customer, we'd made the difficult decision to cancel a workshop—something we don't take lightly—and set out on a potentially dangerous trip back to Ormond Beach. The airlines had canceled all flights into Florida at this point, but we'd managed to get to Atlanta and were making the 425-mile drive south in a rented car with a very worn set of windshield wipers.

As we drove, we maintained a strong safety awareness at all times, but we were scared. Being from Kentucky, we'd seen snowstorms, ice storms, and tornados, but never anything like this. The wind was howling, tree limbs were flying everywhere, and there was an eerie feeling in the air. The most unsettling part was that we were heading into the unknown, only a few hours before the eye of the hurricane was predicted to go through our area.

The storm, luckily, didn't turn out to be as severe as the worst predictions, and our friends and family were unharmed. However, by the time the storm subsided, our neighborhood looked like a war zone. Trees and telephone lines were down, windows were broken, fences were down, roofs were smashed in, and many roads were blocked or washed out. Power and running water were out and didn't return for three days.

Tracey's father and two friends, one of whom was a close-by neighbor, fortunately had enough time to get our storm shutters up before the storm hit. Toyota conditioning had played a part here as well, as I had, in typical 5S fashion, labeled all the shutters with numbers and included a map showing where each shutter went. By following the standardized work I had set up, they were able to get the job done in about 90 minutes without a hitch.

As we helped each other recover from the storm, I had many flashbacks to my Toyota days and how we were conditioned to behave in a crisis. When people were in need, whatever department they were in, you would figure out a way to help them. I remembered how I'd once helped a body weld manager who was struggling through some issues. "Let me know whatever you need," I'd said. "I can support manpower, and I'll figure out whatever I can do to help you through this."

I had a very similar feeling as a group of us shared resources and helped each other recover from the storm. Tracey and I had generators and lots of chargers for people to charge their phones, but we didn't have much gas, so other people shared that with us. We're the only house around with a pool, so we shared water for washing and flushing toilets. A few of us helped a neighbor remove a tree from her roof and find somebody to repair the roof. We let people know we had a satellite phone in case the cellular networks went down. And we were both impressed with how the city did a great job of mobilizing its resources and keeping us all up to date.

It turned out to be a powerful experience for us. The first lesson for me was that you can't understand how important it is to help people in need until you actually experience it. Watching TV, I remember feeling sorry for the people in Hurricane Katrina in New Orleans, but I'd never fully visualized what it's like. Now we understand.

Furthermore, what Toyota taught us about making the group successful, as opposed to just the individual, isn't just about running a company better. It's something that we should apply to our communities as well. When you're in a crisis that's upending people's lives, you really get a strong feeling for that.

Finally, we could really see how the role of conditioning plays out. As we drove into the storm and faced the crisis, the discipline of problem solving was with us the whole time, even when we weren't conscious of it. As we looked around our neighborhood, we saw gaps and thought about how we could fill them.

What the experience shows is that we responded the way we did because of who we are. I didn't set up a work standard for installing the shutters because I had heard this was a "best practice." I did this because that's the way I think. You can see signs of that thinking everywhere in our house. Last Halloween, I was handing out treats in our garage, and a nine-year-old came up to me and said, "I've never seen a garage so well organized." A nine-year-old!

Of course, part of this thinking is improving our standards in case we get another hurricane. This time, we'll have a standard hurricane kit. I've bought some pumps, for example, so we can get gas out of my truck into a can for a generator. I'm also designing a new tool to speed up the installation of the storm shutters. The shutters are secured by wing nuts, and putting on 150 wing nuts by hand takes time. The tool will allow this to be done with a power drill. If you think about it, this is just another example of improving a process.

WE DON'T DO "TRAINING AS USUAL"

When we arrive at a client's location, we are, in many respects, confronting the unknown, just as we were with Hurricane Matthew. We don't know what problems our learners are dealing with, what experiences they've recently had, or what their most pressing needs are. Regardless of how much preparation we do, there's no way of really knowing until we are there.

On the other hand, we have pretty ambitious goals. Because our mandate is to engage our learners in a way of *thinking*, our sessions can't be about "here's an instructor from so and so coming in to teach us"—we have to find a way to connect with each person, and there's no "script" that tells us how to do that.

I think this challenges us to apply our Toyota conditioning from many, many years, and figure out how to best present these ideas to people whose world is very different from a car plant. How do we relate this thinking to their work and their problems?

The process we follow isn't that different from the way we went to *gemba* as leaders. Developing people is all about listening openly and learning about situations through the other person's perspective. We paid close attention to people's different learning styles and made sure we didn't leave any learners behind.

Of course, we have slides and plenty of structured content to help keep the pace, but we're quite comfortable without them.

Often, we go "off script" when the situation dictates. While one of us is presenting, the other will be carefully watching the audience reaction. When we uncover an area where people are confused or uncomfortable, we'll say, "Okay, let's talk about this." Discussions like this led us to develop the Engagement Equation that we outlined in Part 2.

Our sessions involve a lot of hands-on exercises as well, and that's where much of the real learning takes place. Here we go into our role of *gemba* coach that we have practiced for so many years, and during these interactions, we continue to learn.

We also have learned, through our Toyota conditioning, that people's personal lives are highly relevant to their work. On the production line, we often asked team members about their family members as well as about their processes. In our sessions, we always make an effort to get to know a little bit about our learners and their lifestyles. Sometimes they share their culture with us. For example, one of our Canadian clients took us ice fishing—I guess you could say that's a little outside of our Florida comfort zone!

The upshot of all this is that we're learning constantly, just as we did at Toyota. Our customers teach us new ways of approaching our content, and our training keeps evolving. In recent years, for example, we've had some remarkable lessons from organizations that are using Toyota principles in government and healthcare.

The adaptability of these ideas to so many industries shows just how fundamental they are. If you're learning how to handle a crisis, it doesn't matter if the problem is in industry, healthcare, government, finance, or, for that matter, if you're helping neighbors recover from a natural disaster. And although they take a long time to really master, they are accessible to everybody.

Therefore, although the situations our customers are facing are varied and complex, our message is very simple. We were literally homegrown in Toyota's Japanese way of thinking, taught by trainers who could barely speak English. There wasn't much theory—just some simple but very powerful ideas, supported with lots of action-based and example-based learning. This wasn't about Lean or any particular methodology—it was about how to be successful at our jobs.

Since 1988, we have never strayed from the essence of what we were taught back then. This is just the homegrown practicality of two people who learned something, grabbed onto it, grew it, and made it their own. So we don't go into a room and say, "time to perform." This is just what we do because of who we are, and I think that's why people connect with us.

MOVING FORWARD WITH LEAN

Most people in the continuous improvement world will agree that while Lean tools are widely used, most organizations fail to get the culture piece. There are various explanations, but we prefer to look at the issue in the same way we look at any problem—what is the real gap here, and what can leaders do to close that gap?

Unfortunately, most leaders aren't thinking that way. Instead, there's a tendency to think of Lean as a short-term, quick-fix solution for some issue they're having at that moment. And since they are usually relying on lagging indicators, the problem is subjective in the sense that they really don't know what the problem is—they just know they have a problem.

That problem might be affecting a variety of measurements. For example, it can be morale of team members, it can be cost, it can be quality, and there can be a variety of factors influencing each of these. But their lagging indicators often provide little insight into what's actually causing the pain.

So companies will grasp at Lean—maybe they've heard of some success stories in their industry—and say, "Let's do Lean, and we'll be good again." What the lagging indicators don't tell them, however, is that they may never have been very good in the first place. Maybe executives were "making their numbers" and the real problem wasn't an issue for them yet—we see this a lot.

So they're trying to bring back some success they believe they had in the past, with no desire to change the way they think about how they do business every day. Of course, once the lagging indicators aren't looking good, there is all sorts of pressure to turn those around quickly. So companies implement all sorts of reactive measures, and then, perhaps after some initial success, they begin to ask, "Why isn't this working anymore?"

A scenario we see all the time is where a company has been using A3s for a while, at least in terms of practicing the technique, but its people aren't engaging in Go to See, Grasp the Situation, or any of those ways of thinking we've discussed in this book. As a result, they have a number of people mindlessly filling out A3 templates and making little headway in solving the organization's problems. And, I might add, getting pretty frustrated.

At Toyota, our trainers always put the thinking before the methods. For us, it all started with continuous development of people and understanding the "why." Once we'd proven that we understood the thinking, then they would introduce the tools. The point is, if you get the *thinking* down first, the A3 process is very easy to learn and apply.

Many will disagree, but we believe that "fixing things" is not the way to go about Lean. It really needs to start from a genuine desire to change. Somewhere, a light bulb has to go on where the leaders say, "Hey, this reactive thinking is like a treadmill. We're seeing the same problems over and over again, and our people are constantly fighting fires. There's got to be a better way."

Those same people are bound to be disappointed, however, if they expect to find some comfortable steady state in Toyota's methods. The fact is, anybody at Toyota will tell you that they have not arrived anywhere—they are on a journey forever, and they are just as anxious about succeeding as they were a half a century ago. We were learning together the day I started at Toyota, and still learning the day I left.

But most of all, leaders who seek to emulate Toyota must understand how important it is to continuously develop people. To get results from continuous improvement, you have to solve thousands of problems at the *gemba*, and this can't happen without an army of problem solvers. Toyota set the bar here by enlisting its entire workforce, applying what we call Everybody Everyday Engaged (E³).

The fact that humans thrive in such an environment, as we did, makes this a win-win situation where what's good for the company is good for the employee, and vice versa. Fujio Cho summarized this commitment when he said, "First we build people, then we build cars."

THE POWER OF THINKING

The message we emphasize in our training, and have emphasized in this book, is that the *thinking* should always come before the tools, not after. Our trainers followed this approach, and Toyota has never veered from this course—some insiders today are even calling TPS the Thinking Production System. Our thought is that maybe we should call it the Thinking People System!

The Engagement Equation is our summary of the kind of thinking that makes continuous improvement successful. We believe that if people practice these thinking concepts, the learning curve for problem solving will become shorter, results will be stronger, and people will have productive and fulfilling careers.

So we encourage all our readers to embrace the thinking, and to practice it every day. These are powerful concepts that can help you in your work and in your life. They are "thinking tools" that you can carry with you always, whether you are solving a problem at work, pursuing a hobby, or helping friends and neighbors in your community.

So as you move forward, we encourage you to:

- **Go to See.** Get out of your office, get away from your computer, and see for yourself what is happening at the *gemba*. Always know your purpose for going.
- **Grasp the Situation.** Look for facts, and separate them from your assumptions. Where are the measurable gaps between the current and ideal state, and how can we use them to obtain achievable targets?
- **Get to Solution.** Find ways to work with people to get to root causes of problems, and to create and implement plans to remove those root causes from processes.
- **Get to Standardization.** Establish documentation of proven solutions to allow them to be widely shared throughout the organization.
- **Get to Sustainability.** Monitor the processes for stability, watch leading indicators, and always be ready to change the standards when they are no longer valid.
- **Get to Stretch.** Develop people continuously, and challenge them to constantly raise the bar by improving the standards.

Then, once you've mastered these concepts, lead others in this way of thinking until everybody in the organization is engaged in it every day.

This is discipline and accountability, our own DNA. We're confident that if you learn to think this way, you will be successful in everything you do.

Good luck, and as we say on the back of our business card, *go thinking!*

Index